The Pressure
Cooker Cookbook

The Pressure
Cooker Cookbook

Catherine Phipps

over 150 simple, essential,
time-saving recipes

EBURY
PRESS

1 3 5 7 9 10 8 6 4 2

Published in 2012 by Ebury Press, an imprint of Ebury Publishing

A Random House Group Company

The Random House Group Limited Reg. No. 954009

Addresses for companies within the Random House Group can be found at www.randomhouse.co.uk

A CIP catalogue record for this book is available from the British Library

Photographer: Dan Jones
Food styling: Catherine Phipps and Emma Marsden
Props styling: Jessica Georgiades
Design: Lucy Stephens
Editor: Ione Walder

The Random House Group Limited supports The Forest Stewardship Council® (FSC®), the leading international forest certification organisation. Our books carrying the FSC label are printed on FSC® certified paper. FSC is the only forest certification scheme endorsed by the leading environmental organisations, including Greenpeace. Our paper procurement policy can be found at www.randomhouse.co.uk/environment

To buy books by your favourite authors and register for offers visit www.randomhouse.co.uk

Printed and bound in China by Toppan Leefung

ISBN 9780091945015

MIX
Paper from
responsible sources
FSC
www.fsc.org   FSC® C104723

Contents

To Shariq

Introduction

'I now can't imagine cooking without one. The benefits are enormous. Most cooking times are reduced by a huge 70 per cent with no sacrifice to taste'

Why Pressure Cookers?

A few years ago, I had an almost Damascene conversion to cooking with pressure cookers. Until then, I had held quite a negative view of them – were they not old-fashioned, noisy, dangerous beasties, belching out steam and terrorising our mothers and grandmothers with a constant threat of explosion?

Well, no. At least, not any more. I started to take them seriously on the day I watched my Brazilian sister-in-law use a pressure cooker to produce a delicious meal of black beans with sausages (see my version of her recipe on page 122). The beans were dry and unsoaked, yet the dish was on the table in just over half an hour. This seemed miraculous to me, so it wasn't long before I'd bought my own cooker and started experimenting. I soon discovered that today's models are very different from the sort I had grown up with. They are sleek, stainless steel and highly efficient, with numerous safety features.

I now can't imagine cooking without one. The benefits are enormous. The mere fact that most cooking times are reduced by a huge 70 per cent is enough, but think of what else that means. These days, when we are all short of time, when we are battling with escalating fuel bills (at the time of writing my supplier had just put mine up by 18 per cent) and rising food prices, as well as being put under pressure (no pun intended) to cut our carbon emissions, a pressure cooker is an invaluable tool. Not only does it save you time and fuel, but it means that you can save money by buying cheap cuts of meat and dried goods instead of tinned, and not have to worry that you are spending a small fortune having to cook them slowly. They have known this in the developing world for a long time, which is why almost every home in Central Asia and South America has one.

Another reason why pressure cookers are popular in hot climates is because they keep kitchens cooler by cutting cooking times and minimising oven use. So while they are particularly good with all those winter foods (stews, casseroles, steamed puddings), they are also ideal for summer use. They can speed up the process of preserving, and I even use mine to make food for picnics, salads and light, summery puddings. You can also use them outdoors. If I were the sort of person who enjoyed camping, I couldn't imagine anything more useful to take with me – you'd be able to make your campfire or portable gas ring go much further.

Most importantly to me as a lover of good food, there is no sacrifice to taste. If there is one myth I would like to dispel about pressure cookers, it would be this. There is no compromise necessary; taste and texture will always be as good – in fact, in some instances the food actually tastes better. Some of our most respected chefs cottoned on to this a while ago. If Heston Blumenthal thinks that pressure cooker stocks and sauces are superior to those made conventionally, who are we to argue? The number of chefs who now admit to using a pressure cooker in their kitchens is growing, on both sides of the Atlantic, and they are even cropping up on popular cooking shows and competitions. People have finally realised that using a pressure cooker hugely increases one's options, especially when you are short of time. And it's not all about tough cuts of meat and pulses. You will find recipes here that speed up braising, steaming, sautéeing, pot roasting, even baking and double boiling (using the pressure cooker as a *bain marie*).

I am influenced by all kinds of things in my cooking – friends and family, places I have lived, and simply what food is available to me locally, but most of all by the need to feed a hungry, growing family without resorting to convenience foods. These influences are reflected in my recipes, which I hope will show you how versatile the pressure cooker can be. Along the way I've also attempted to give you hints and tips on how to convert your own favourite recipes for the pressure cooker. These days, my pressure cooker takes up permanent residence on the hob, because it is a rare day when it isn't used in some way. I hope that the recipes in this book will go some way to encouraging you to use yours just as much.

How to Use Your Pressure Cooker Safely

The principle behind pressure cooking is quite a simple one. Basically, the pressure cooker's lid is weighted down and sealed with a gasket, which means that steam is prevented from escaping. The steam builds up in the cooker, increasing the pressure and therefore the temperature, which will exceed boiling point and cook the food at around 122°C when the pressure is at its highest, reducing cooking times by about two-thirds.

In the bad old days, when pressure cookers had a fearsome reputation, pressure would build up and cookers would jiggle around alarmingly and very occasionally – this is the stuff urban myths are made of – explode! This doesn't happen these days as modern pressure cookers have many safety features, not least more than one safety valve to ensure that excess steam can be safely and automatically released when necessary.

This does not mean you should be cavalier in your treatment of your pressure cooker! Some basic, common-sense guidelines should be followed:

1. Always read the user manual and follow the instructions on how to operate and maintain your cooker. Pay particular attention to the safety features – you will need to oil the rubber gasket regularly and check for splits, and the valves need checking for blockages, especially after cooking anything that foams (starchy foods such as pasta and pulses).

2. Never force the pressure cooker open before the pressure has completely dropped. I stupidly, if deliberately, tried this once to see what would happen and ended up with a scalded hand and boiling water all over the floor. If the pressure gauge is still up, the contents of the cooker will still be cooking at pressure, which means that any liquids will be fiercely boiling.

3. When releasing pressure, always make sure that the cooker is tilting slightly away from you, so as to avoid getting a faceful of steam. The steam can be hot enough to scald so do be careful.

4. Do not leave your pressure cooker unattended!

Which Pressure Cooker?

These days there are numerous pressure cookers to choose from – they vary enormously in terms of price and quality, from standard aluminium to sleek stainless-steel models with all kinds of safety valves and visual pressure gauges. During the course of writing this book, I tried around a dozen different kinds, including electric models. I am happy using most of them, but have my preferences of course. I always find myself reaching for either a WMF or Fissler model, which really are top of the range. However, the keenly priced Prestige is also a very reliable option. If you haven't yet bought a pressure cooker (and I really hope this book encourages you to do so), here are a few things you should consider before deciding which one to buy.

Size Matters

Many pressure cooker manufacturers say that a 4- or 4.5-litre capacity cooker is a good all-rounder and large enough for a regular family's needs. This is for the most part true. However, I would say that if you really want to maximise your savings in terms of time and fuel, the next size up (6 or 6.5 litres) is a much better purchase. It is not much more expensive to buy and you will have the advantage of being able to cook double quantities of all sorts of things. This means that you can effectively cook more than one meal at a time or cook in bulk to stock up the

freezer. You will also be able to make larger quantities of stock – not many beef bones will fit into a 4-litre pot.

The second point about size concerns dimension. Go for a wider model if possible. It will make life easier when browning meat (especially chicken – turning a whole bird in a high-sided pressure cooker is not the easiest of manoeuvres). It will also hold several ramekins without having to stack them up, and will fit a cake tin more easily. Depth is less of a consideration – the tallest thing you are likely to put into it is a pudding basin and these will fit easily into all 4-litre+ models.

PSI

This is the measurement of weight (pounds per square inch), which tells you what pressure your cooker operates at. Try to make sure you get a cooker which specifies 14–16 PSI, as anything lower will require longer cooking times and make following the recipes in this or any other pressure cooker book quite tricky.

Liquid

Most manufacturers specify a minimum amount of water that you should add to the cooker. While I don't think this is something that should always be followed to the letter (see, for instance, some of the recipes in the Vegetables chapter on page 161), a model that requires a lower liquid minimum is more versatile. This is an advantage because you will be able to braise vegetables and meat with less liquid, meaning that your vegetables will not become waterlogged and there will be less need to reduce down any remaining cooking liquor.

Noise and Steam Emissions

Some models are noisier than others, there's no doubt about that. The quieter models are virtually silent when pressure is reached. This is partly because they don't emit steam when cooking at pressure. This, incidentally, has an additional benefit – because less steam is released during the cooking process, you will need to add less liquid and the flavours will concentrate in the pressure cooker rather than escaping into your kitchen.

All About Pressure

Setting Pressure

All pressure cookers allow you to cook at an approximation of low and high pressure. Some also have regular steam settings. Some models allow you to select which pressure you require by setting a dial, others simply show which pressure has been reached via a visual indicator. I do not like the dial system, purely because too often I forget to set it.

Maintaining Pressure

When your cooker has reached the required pressure, you will find that a minimal amount of heat is needed to maintain this. I normally start off on a large gas ring and move the cooker over to a smaller one once pressure has been reached. It will take a bit of trial and error to work out how much heat you need to maintain this pressure, as every cooker is different, but you will very quickly get the hang of it.

Releasing Pressure

Most modern pressure cookers have a fast pressure-release mechanism, which operates by simply turning a dial. A few exceptions require you to press down on the temperature gauge in the centre of the lid. You have to do this with a wooden spoon or protect your hand with a glove because you will be releasing hot steam; needless to say, this is not my preferred method.

Useful Equipment

To get the best out of this book and from your pressure cooker, there are a few pieces of equipment which will be useful, most of which you will no doubt already have.

Your pressure cooker should come with at least one trivet and a steamer basket. The trivet is useful for balancing large items on, but not at all practical for smaller receptacles such as ramekins. These should be placed in the steamer basket instead.

Timer

This is the single most important thing you will need when using the pressure cooker, as many of the timings, especially for vegetables, are very precise.

Cooking Receptacles

There are quite a few recipes in this book that involve using the pressure cooker as a *bain marie* (water bath) or steamer. For these you will need a selection of ovenproof dishes, ramekins and pudding basins. I tend to use ceramic or Pyrex dishes. Pyrex bowls are particularly good for things like lemon curd or custard (see pages 190 and 210). It is perfectly safe to use plastic in the pressure cooker – the plastic bowls with lids that you can now get are very convenient to use for making steamed puddings, as there is no need to make a lid out of foil or greaseproof paper.

Tea Towels

Sometimes the item I need to put in the pressure cooker is a bit too tall to sit in the steamer basket. Instead, I put a folded-up piece of old tea towel in the base of the cooker. This avoids any receptacle coming into direct contact with the base of the pressure cooker. I should say that nothing bad would happen if you didn't use the tea towel, but things do have a tendency to rattle around, which can be a bit on the noisy side.

Elastic Bands

For sealing foil or baking parchment on pudding basins and smaller receptacles, strong elastic bands are very useful and much more convenient to use than string. My postman has a seemingly endless supply of red ones that he posts through my letter box!

Heat Diffusion Mat

If, like me, you have a hob that will not hold a consistently low temperature, you may find it difficult to cook those (admittedly few) dishes that need cooking at low as opposed to high pressure. A heat diffusion mat is invaluable here – otherwise you will find yourself constantly having to move your pressure cooker on and off the heat.

Foil and Greaseproof Paper

When I first started using a pressure cooker, I used a lot of foil, but eventually realised that it slows down cooking times quite considerably. Now, I mainly use it for fish, suet rolls (see page 79) and steamed puddings (see pages 186 and 188). Almost everything else is better with greaseproof paper, and in fact, I've come to realise that quite a lot of things don't need covering at all.

Foil is useful, however, for making a handle with which to lower things in and out of the pressure cooker. This is particularly necessary for anything that is quite a snug fit, as it would otherwise require a degree of dexterity that I certainly don't possess. Take a long sheet of foil and fold it in half twice lengthways, so that it is four-ply and a quarter of its original width – this will make it extremely sturdy. You can then use it as a 'handle' by placing any receptacle centrally on top of it, then holding both sides of the foil to manoeuvre things in and out of the pressure cooker. Once your receptacle is in the cooker, simply fold down the edges of the foil to fit inside, and unroll again after cooking, ready to lift out.

Food Processor/Blender

Some kind of food processor would also be useful. I recommend using a hand blender, which is brilliant for puréeing soups in situ without having to transfer them into a jug blender. Most come with attachments that allow you to easily chop vegetables, make breadcrumbs for stuffings and pastes for curries, and grind spices. I find mine indispensable.

A Note on Recipes and Ingredients

All quantities serve four people unless otherwise stated.

All the eggs used in the recipes are large unless otherwise stated.

All spoon measurements are rounded.

Butter is always unsalted.

Vegetables are always medium-sized unless otherwise stated.

All onions, garlic, root ginger, potatoes and root vegetables are peeled unless otherwise stated.

Vegetables should always be washed before use.

Unless the recipe specifies otherwise, a bouquet garni consists of two bay leaves and sprigs of curly parsley and thyme. You can either tie these together with butcher's twine, wrap and tie in leek leaves or, if including spices, wrap in muslin.

Many of my recipes start with a combination of olive oil and butter. I love the flavour of butter and the olive oil stops it from burning and browning quickly. Feel free to substitute this combination with any kind of vegetable oil or fat if you prefer.

Timings are given from the moment the cooker reaches the desired pressure. Wherever I give an estimate, err on the side of caution and go with the shorter time initially, especially with fish, fruit and vegetable dishes. You can always return to pressure or simmer if things aren't cooked, but overcooked food is much harder to salvage.

I specify whether you should let the pressure in your cooker drop immediately (fast release) or gradually (slow or natural release). Slow or natural release simply requires you to remove the cooker from the heat and wait for the pressure gauge to drop. With fast release you have a couple of options – you can follow the instructions as set out by each individual manufacturer, or you can run cold water over the lid of the cooker. Only use the cold water method where specified.

I include several recipes for curry powders and pastes and also use quite a lot of whole spices. If you prefer to use commercial blends, I recommend Shan brand for my mother-in-law's Pakistani recipes, Mae Ploy for Thai curries, Seasoned Pioneer blends, and The Spice Shop in Notting Hill (who have an online shop) as they do whole spice blends as well as ground.

Soups and Stocks

'A well-flavoured stock provides you with the basis for so many different meals'

If you are going to make anything in the pressure cooker, a soup or stock is a good place to start. A well-flavoured stock provides you with the basis for so many different meals, including many soups. As for soups – there are few things that are as easy to make, and once you start making them in the pressure cooker, they're quicker too. Making a soup from scratch rather than reaching for a tin of Heinz is a much more realistic proposition when you can cut the cooking time down so significantly. There is rarely an occasion when I don't have cartons of home-made soup in the fridge or freezer and it's my default lunch, whatever the weather.

Hopefully the recipes here will give you good enough guidance to soon be able to adapt your own favourite soups for the pressure cooker and you'll never need to cook them conventionally again.

Stocks

Making stock is one of those things that many people feel is far too much of a faff to do regularly. This is a shame, because even the most simple stock (think any flavoured cooking water, even the liquid in which you've just cooked some vegetables), can help to add depth of flavour to your finished dish, and in some cases (especially in the case of risotto) stock is absolutely essential.

Stocks are building blocks. As well as adding them to soups, risottos and a host of other dishes in this book, you can transform them into any number of broths. Think of the British beef tea, consommés or clear soups such as French onion and the medicinal chicken noodle, cleansing hot and sour soups from the Far East, Vietnamese Pho, and Korean or Japanese Dashi. You can cook noodles in soups, break eggs into them or heat them up for Mongolian or Chinese takes on fondue – the possibilities are endless.

I was initially sceptical about pressure cooker stock, put off by tales of cloudy, sour-tasting liquor tainting any dish that was unfortunate enough to be touched by it. I assumed that it was a poor substitute for The Real Thing. Fortunately, I was put right. First, when I was interviewing Marguerite Patten for an article, she quite firmly told me that any nasty-tasting pressure-cooked stock was the result of inferior, less-than-fresh ingredients and overcooking. Then I came across some of Heston Blumenthal's numerous writings on pressure cookers – he unequivocally states that pressure cooker stock is vastly superior to anything made conventionally.

After such endorsements, I had to try for myself – I haven't made stock conventionally since and I am in no doubt that pressure cooker stock is indeed hard to beat, as long as you follow these simple rules.

1. Make sure your ingredients are fresh. By all means economise – I keep a bag of clean vegetable peelings, etc., in the freezer for when I need to make a batch, but nothing past its prime goes in.

2. For better clarity, always start with cold water.

3. When you have brought your water to the boil, always skim off the mushroom-grey scum that collects on the top, until it turns white. You won't always get this scum – it's more common with red meat and game stocks.

4. Do not overcook; be precise with the timings given.

5. Strain the stock through a double layer of muslin.

6. If you can, chill the stock before you use it; this ensures that any fat will go solid and sit on the top, making it very easy to remove.

There are numerous types of stock that work well with the recipes in this book. I am quite obsessive about them (at one time, when I had a bigger freezer than the one I have now, I had around a dozen different types to hand).

Poultry and Meat Stocks

The principles for these stocks remain the same, regardless of what kind of meat you are using. There are two basic kinds of meat-based stocks – a rich, brown version, or a paler, more delicate infusion. If you want the former, it is best first to roast or brown the bones and meat that you are using.

The main difference between those stocks made from poultry and those made from red meat is that you tend to get more meat left on the carcass of a bird (especially on small game birds where the spindly little legs are often left untouched), obviating the need to add additional meat to the pot. For a red meat stock, I sometimes find that a bit of additional meat is necessary to add a layer to the flavour.

The stock I make most often is chicken. I poach a whole chicken in water and aromatics (20 minutes at high pressure, then natural release) and use the resultant broth. (See also the Poached Chicken recipe on page 85). I save any chicken carcasses and bones in a bag in the freezer until I have enough to make a stock – and sometimes I supplement the bones with a few wings, or the trays of chicken backs that I can buy at my local farmers' market (it is worth looking out for these, they are as cheap as chips). The same applies to duck and game birds. A duck provides much, as you can also reserve the fat, and use the carcass for a lovely, rich stock that is wonderful used in any wintry soups or with robust grains such as barley and spelt (see the barley and spelt risottos on pages 158–9). Incidentally, the poaching method also works with meat – it is how I cook a ham hock (see page 69).

Regarding aromatics, you can add whatever flavours you like. I usually omit anything too hotly spiced, such as chilli or ginger, because they tend to overpower – they are best added to the main dish instead.

For poultry stock

1kg raw chicken/duck/game bones or a mixture of raw and cooked carcasses

For meat stock

750g bones (if beef, try to get marrow bones)

250g lean, tough meat with good connective tissue, such as shin

For both types of stock

1 onion, cut into quarters
2 carrots, roughly chopped
1 celery stick, roughly chopped
3–4 leek tops

1 tsp black peppercorns
2 bay leaves
1 parsley sprig

Optional additions

A few unpeeled garlic cloves
Pared citrus zest or kaffir lime leaves
More whole herb sprigs, such as tarragon or thyme

Other aromatics, such as star anise, allspice or juniper berries (all good with duck or game birds)

If you want a dark stock, put the bones in the base of the pressure cooker (no need to add fat) and sear on all sides until they are nicely browned. Then cover with 1.5 litres of cold water, bring to the boil and skim as described on page 19, before adding all the remaining ingredients. Close the lid and bring to high pressure. If you are using bones that have already been cooked (i.e. a chicken carcass), cook for 30 minutes. If you are using raw bones (even if you have browned them first), cook for 45 minutes. Allow to drop pressure naturally. Strain the stock through two layers of muslin and chill until the fat has set on top. Remove this (you can use it in your cooking). Your stock is now ready to use, or you can simmer over a high heat to reduce it down and concentrate the flavour – it is worth doing this for at least some of your stock as this is very useful for adding to gravies. The stock will keep for up to a week in the fridge, or at least three months in the freezer.

Vegetable Stock

The simplest type of vegetable stock comes from steaming vegetables in the pressure cooker. Some of the flavour and nutrients will end up in the water, and this delicately flavoured liquid can supplement the other liquids you use in vegetarian soups and risottos, or can even be added to your pasta sauces in place of water. If you want more flavour, simply add aromatics – this will flavour both the water and the vegetables that you are cooking. I like to add slices of ginger when steaming broccoli or greens, or tarragon or mint to new potatoes (the cooking liquid from potatoes is a good stock to use for soups, as the starch is a natural thickener).

You can also make simple stocks from vegetable discards. If you have pods from fresh peas, you can cook them by covering with cold water, bringing to high pressure and immediately removing from the heat, then allowing them to drop pressure naturally. Do the same with the woody stems of asparagus, or put the two together.

My regular vegetable stock includes an onion, carrot and celery stick, along with any other bits and pieces I have available. Fennel trimmings are good, as are the skin and fibrous strands from squashes and pumpkins. I normally add some herbs, black peppercorns and fennel seed as well. For colour and extra umami flavour (meaning intensely savoury and now considered to be the fifth of our basic tastes) you can also add tomato skins and seeds, and mushroom trimmings.

Cook for a scant 5 minutes under high pressure, then allow to drop pressure naturally and strain immediately. The stock will keep for up to a week in the fridge, or at least three months in the freezer.

Fish Stock

Use fish bones, heads and skin along with herbs and vegetables, and use double the weight of water to bones. I often add aniseedy flavours – fennel, dill, parsley, tarragon – as they all work particularly well with fish, as do citrus notes, particularly lime, orange and lemongrass. You can also make a court-bouillon, which is a stronger-flavoured broth. Simply use half water, half white wine: this is a lovely basis for a fish soup or to use as a poaching liquid. Also, don't forget to include the shells and heads of crustaceans – whether cooked or uncooked, they make a good stock and can even be blitzed afterwards to make a very frugal version of bisque.

Bring to the boil and skim as described on page 19, then close the lid and cook at high pressure for 5 minutes. Allow to drop pressure naturally. This stock will keep only for a couple of days in the fridge, or a maximum of 3 months in the freezer.

Summer Chicken Soup

This soup is based on a memory of a cold, wet day, 13 years ago, when I'd struggled into college with a horrendous flu bug. My husband, who was at that time a fellow student, coaxed me to eat a bowl of chicken, lemon and tarragon soup before making sure I got home safely, and it's been one of my favourite soups ever since. This is my version of it.

40g butter

1 leek, finely chopped

2 small waxy potatoes, finely diced

2 garlic cloves, finely chopped

1 lemongrass stalk, tough outer layers removed, inner part finely chopped

2 kaffir lime leaves (optional)

150g diced chicken (I prefer thighs, but breast is fine)

Bunch of tarragon, leaves and stems separated

600ml chicken or vegetable stock

Grated zest and juice of 1 lemon or lime

2 tsp soy sauce

150ml double cream

Salt and freshly ground pepper

Melt the butter in the pressure cooker. Add the leek and potatoes and cook over a very low heat just to get the cooking process going.

Meanwhile, make a paste from the garlic, lemongrass and lime leaves, if using – easiest done with a little water in a small food processor or pestle and mortar, else just chop them as finely as you possibly can. Add this paste to the pressure cooker along with the chicken and tarragon stems. Stir for a couple of minutes, pour in all the stock, season with salt and pepper and close the lid.

Bring to high pressure and cook for 2 minutes only. Fast release. Fish out the tarragon stems, then add the citrus zest and juice, soy sauce and double cream and simmer gently until everything is combined. Finely chop the tarragon leaves and add just before serving.

Minestrone

Although everyone has their own version of this classic, it's worth including purely to illustrate how quick and easy it is in the pressure cooker, with no detriment to flavour. It is, of course, infinitely adaptable (one of those 'anything goes' soups that will soak up any vegetables you need to use up), so follow this recipe as a rough guide rather than to the letter. I always use a well-flavoured chicken stock, and perhaps will throw in a ham bone, raw or cooked, and Parmesan rind saved in the freezer just for this soup. The overall flavour will be better the following day, so do consider making enough for leftovers. Other good things to add at the end include sliced courgettes or a cupful of peas. To turn it into Minestrone alla Genovese, stir pesto into individual bowls prior to serving.

125g dried borlotti or cannellini beans (or 250g cooked, or a 400g tin)

1 bay leaf (unless using cooked beans)

2 tbsp vegetable oil (unless using cooked beans)

2 tbsp olive oil

100g bacon or pancetta, cut into lardons

1 large onion, sliced

2 carrots, cut on the diagonal

2 celery sticks, cut on the diagonal

1 fennel bulb, trimmed and sliced

3 garlic cloves, finely chopped

Large bunch of Swiss chard, leaves and stems separated, leaves shredded

100g broad beans, blanched and peeled if old

100ml red wine

50g broken-up spaghetti or small pasta shapes

750ml chicken stock or water

4 tomatoes, peeled and chopped, or 200g tinned

1 Parmesan rind (of any size)

Bouquet garni (see page 16) of thyme, bay and flat-leaf parsley

50g grated Parmesan or Grana Padano

Salt and freshly ground pepper

If you are cooking your beans from scratch, put them in the pressure cooker and fill with water up to the halfway mark. Add the bay leaf and the vegetable oil. Close the lid and bring to high pressure. Cook for 25 minutes, then release quickly. The beans will probably be a little *al dente*, but will finish cooking in the soup. Drain and set aside.

Heat the olive oil in the pressure cooker and add the bacon lardons. When they have browned, add the onion, carrots, celery, fennel, garlic and Swiss chard stems and fry for a couple of minutes over quite a high heat until everything starts taking on colour. Return the beans to the pressure cooker, along with all the remaining ingredients, except the grated Parmesan. Season with salt and pepper. Close the lid, bring to high pressure and cook for 5 minutes, then allow to release pressure slowly.

Check the seasoning and add the grated cheese. Fish out the Parmesan rind unless you will be reheating some or all of the soup at a later date. (I have been known to fish out and refreeze the rind until the next time I need it.) Serve piping hot.

Spiced Oxtail Soup

This is the soup version of a Caribbean casserole that I make. (For the casserole, I also add broad beans. If you'd prefer to make the casserole, use just 250ml stock and simmer some broad beans in it when reheating.) The butter and sugar combination in which the meat is cooked might seem unusual, and when you've added the spices and the alcohol you might feel as though you are cooking your oxtail in butterbeer, but trust me, the end result is good. The soup or casserole will be much better the next day, when you will have the added benefit of being able to remove the fat more easily.

½ tsp aniseed (whole or ground)

½ tsp allspice berries (or ground)

1 tsp black peppercorns (or ground)

1 tbsp flour

1 large oxtail, approx. 1.5kg, cut widthways into 4–5cm sections

2 tbsp butter

1 tsp brown sugar

1 tbsp rum

250ml light beer

2 fat garlic cloves, crushed

½ Scotch bonnet pepper, seeded and finely chopped

2 large carrots, cut into small chunks

1 onion, roughly chopped

2 celery sticks, roughly chopped

100g chopped tomatoes (tinned is fine)

1 litre stock (preferably beef)

1 bay leaf

1 thyme sprig

Salt

Port or Madeira, to serve

Grind the aniseed, allspice and black pepper together (unless you are using ready-ground spices) and mix with the flour. Pat the oxtail dry with kitchen towel, then rub the spice mix over the pieces.

Heat the butter and sugar in the pressure cooker until they have melted together. Do not overcook or they will impart a very unpleasant flavour to your soup. Add the oxtail and fry until brown – by this time everything should smell very sweetly spiced. Pour in the rum and wait for the spluttering and hissing to subside before pouring over the beer. Add all the remaining ingredients, then season with salt. Close the lid and bring to high pressure. Cook for 45 minutes then allow to drop pressure naturally.

Remove the oxtail pieces from the cooker and strain everything else through a sieve, pushing as much of the vegetables through as possible, as this will help thicken the soup. When the oxtail is cool enough to handle, remove all the meat from the bones and discard the bones and any large pieces of fat. Return the meat to the liquid.

If possible, chill overnight so that the fat can be easily removed – this will also improve the flavour no end. Otherwise, allow to cool a little and carefully spoon off the fat. If you like, add a little glug of port or Madeira just before serving.

Harira

I have lost count of the number of times I have made this soup. I first came across it in one of the Two Fat Ladies' books, years before I became interested in Moroccan food, and I have always come back to it, as for me, the combinations of different textures are just right. My recipe is based upon their version, but I have just changed the spice mix a little. If you want to make this soup quickly, use pre-cooked chickpeas (see the instructions on page 132) or use a 400g tin.

115g dried chickpeas (or 250g cooked, or a 400g tin)
1 tbsp olive oil
25g butter
1 large onion, finely chopped
350g lamb, preferably neck fillet or shoulder, cut into 3cm cubes
2 garlic cloves, finely chopped

1 tsp ground ginger
1 tsp turmeric
1 tsp ground cumin
½ tsp cayenne pepper
¼ tsp ground cinnamon
1 litre chicken stock
Generous pinch of saffron
400g tin of chopped tomatoes

55g long-grain rice
2 red peppers, skinned, seeded and cut into thick strips
Juice of 1 lemon
1 tbsp finely chopped flat-leaf parsley
Salt and freshly ground pepper

If you need to cook your chickpeas, do this first, following the instructions on page 132.

Heat the oil and butter in the base of the pressure cooker. Add the onion and sauté until starting to soften, then turn up the heat a little, add the lamb and brown on all sides. Add the garlic and spices and fry for a couple of minutes more. Pour over the chicken stock, season with salt and pepper, then close the lid. Bring to high pressure, cook for 15 minutes, then fast release.

Put the saffron in 2 tablespoons of warm water to infuse, then add this to the pressure cooker along with the tomatoes, rice and cooked chickpeas. Close the lid, bring to high pressure again and cook for a further 5 minutes. Allow to release pressure naturally, then add the red peppers and lemon juice. Allow to simmer for a couple of minutes and top up with a little water or stock if you feel it needs it. Serve sprinkled with the parsley.

Lentil and Swiss Chard Soup

This is based on a Lebanese soup, Adas Bi Hamud. The proof of the pudding is in the eating, but this applies to soup too. When I lived in Norfolk and was involved with the wonderful people who run Aylsham's Slow Food convivium, we held a pudding night. This was the soup I offered as an appetiser. It went down extremely well – not a drop left and people returning for seconds and thirds, despite their keenness to get on with sampling the thirty-odd puddings on offer! You can use a good vegetable or chicken stock with this recipe but I usually use water.

300g Swiss chard, leaves and stems separated
2 tbsp olive oil
1 red onion, halved and sliced lengthways
4 garlic cloves, finely chopped
50g fresh coriander, leaves roughly chopped, stems finely chopped
250g red lentils, well rinsed
1 litre stock or water
1 tbsp ground cumin
2 tsp ground coriander
½ tsp ground cinnamon
½ tsp mild chilli powder
Juice of 1 lemon
Salt and freshly ground pepper

Shred the Swiss chard leaves and chop the stems into 1cm pieces, keeping the two separate.

Heat the olive oil in the base of the pressure cooker. Add the onion and the chard stems and fry until starting to take on some colour. Add the garlic and coriander stems, cook for another minute, then add the lentils and the stock or water. Take a little of the liquid and mix it with all the spices, then add to the pressure cooker. Season with salt and pepper. Close the lid and bring to high pressure. Cook for 5 minutes only, then fast release.

Stir in the shredded chard leaves and the coriander leaves and simmer until the chard has wilted. When you are about to serve, pour in the lemon juice. Check the seasoning and add more salt, pepper or lemon juice if you like.

Root Vegetable and Game Soup

You could use this recipe as a template for any soup containing root vegetables, as the quantities and cooking times will be the same. I specify game stock because I think that its strong, savoury flavour works particularly well with sweet root vegetables, especially parsnips, but please use whatever kind of stock you like. A good garnish for this soup is any crisp, shredded game meat or perhaps even their offal if you have them (heart, kidneys, liver), flash-fried and sizzled in a little sherry.

50g butter

2 garlic cloves, finely chopped

1 medium onion, chopped

500g parsnips or other root vegetables, diced

100g floury potatoes, diced

Bouquet garni (see page 16) of bay, thyme and parsley

1 litre well-flavoured game stock

100ml single cream (optional)

Squeeze of lemon juice

Finely chopped curly parsley, to garnish

Salt and freshly ground pepper

Heat the butter in the base of the pressure cooker over a medium heat, then add the garlic and all the vegetables. Sauté briskly for a few minutes until everything starts to soften around the edges and take on a golden-brown colour. Throw in the bouquet garni and pour over the stock. Season generously with salt and pepper. Close the lid and bring to high pressure. Cook for 3 minutes, then release the pressure naturally.

Allow to cool a little, then purée until smooth and creamy. Add the cream if you want additional richness, along with a squeeze of lemon juice and more salt and pepper to taste. Serve sprinkled with finely chopped parsley.

Caribbean Smoked Ham and Red Lentil Soup

This recipe calls for ham stock, preferably made from boiling a ham hock. If this isn't possible, you can either add a ham bone to the soup while cooking, add a 100g piece of uncooked smoked ham to the pot and shred at the end, or even just fry some lardons of bacon along with the vegetables at the start.

Please take note of the advice about bagging up the Scotch bonnet pepper. I once served this soup to a spice-phobic septuagenarian who ended with a whole mouthful of disintegrating hot pepper and was very upset.

I often serve this soup with a large dollop of mango chutney stirred in, to achieve a nice contrast of sweet and salty.

---

2 tbsp vegetable oil
1 large onion, finely diced
2 carrots, finely diced
2 celery sticks, finely diced
½ butternut squash, finely diced

1 red pepper, finely diced
250g red lentils, well rinsed
1 thyme sprig
2 bay leaves
1 tsp allspice berries

1 Scotch bonnet pepper, left whole but pricked with a knife tip
1 litre smoked ham stock or water
Salt and freshly ground pepper

Heat the oil in the base of the pressure cooker and add all the vegetables. Sauté for a few minutes until the vegetables start to take on a little colour, then add the lentils.

Make a bouquet garni (see page 16) with the thyme, bay leaves, allspice and Scotch bonnet pepper. (This is most easily done by placing them all in a square piece of muslin and tying it up with string. But you can skip this step if you don't mind fishing out the aromatics individually after cooking.) Add this to the pressure cooker and pour in the stock or water. Do not add salt at this point – smoked ham is quite salty.

Close the lid and bring up to full pressure. Cook for 5 minutes then allow the pressure to release naturally. Stir the soup briskly as some of the lentils will be floating on top, then check for seasoning. Leave the bouquet garni in the soup until you are ready to serve.

Cucumber Soup

This is just the soup you need at the height of summer, when cucumbers are plentiful and you are running out of ideas for using them. I started making this one year when just one plant in my greenhouse yielded about 50 large cucumbers. These days I prefer smaller ones or the 'crooks' found in Middle Eastern shops as they have more flavour than the watery supermarket offerings. The soup is light, refreshing and equally good hot or chilled. It's worth making in the pressure cooker because cucumbers take a surprisingly long time to soften.

I have two garnishes to suggest here. Firstly, some well-seasoned cooked crab meat, dressed with lime juice. Alternatively, for a much zestier contrast to the soothing cucumber soup, try borage oil or pesto (see the recipe below).

40g butter
1 leek, finely chopped
150g potatoes, diced
600g cucumbers, half of
 them peeled, all cut in half

lengthways then into chunks
750ml vegetable stock, or half
 chicken stock/half water
1 large tarragon sprig
½cm piece of root ginger

3cm strip of pared lime zest
Squeeze of lime juice
Salt and ground white pepper

Melt the butter in the base of the pressure cooker then add the leek, potatoes and cucumber. Sauté for 2–3 minutes, until everything is glossy with butter. Add the stock or stock/water combination and season with salt and pepper. Make a bouquet garni (see page 16) with the tarragon, ginger and lime zest and add this too.

Close the lid, bring up to high pressure and cook for 5 minutes. Allow to release slowly. Fish out the bouquet garni, then purée the rest. Return the bouquet garni to the cooker until you are ready to serve. Squeeze over some lime juice and serve garnished with crab meat (see introduction) or borage oil or pesto (see below).

Borage Oil or Pesto

Edible flowers are really becoming popular again. This idea comes from Frances Bissell's *The Scented Garden* and she has kindly agreed to let me reproduce her recipe for borage oil here. For borage pesto, replace the basil in any pesto recipe with borage leaves.

3 tbsp borage flowers,
 blue petals only

¼ tsp sea salt

6 tbsp sunflower oil

Put the petals in a mortar with the sea salt and pound to a paste (you can use a food processor). Gradually add the oil, ensuring that the liquid is well amalgamated. Mix it again before serving. Spoon over soup or drizzle through a plastic bottle.

Creamed Endive and Cheese Soup

Endive, chicory, *witloof* – these pale-yellow torpedoes provoke extreme love/ hate reactions in people, mainly because of their bitterness. I love them, so use them a lot at home, either braised or gratinéed (see recipe on page 174), or in this soup which is rich and creamy with enough bitterness from the endive to give it character. It is very good garnished with some fried, crumbled bacon or some crisp, shredded pork.

If you want to temper the bitterness of the endive (not everyone does), I have a tip for you, gleaned from the wonderful Spanish cookbook *1080 Recipes*. Put your prepared endive into a pan of cold, salted water and set over a high heat. As soon as the water comes to the boil, remove the endive and plunge into another pan of cold, salted water. I have found that blanching it in this way is sufficient. If you don't want to curb the bitterness, you can sauté the raw chicory along with the onion and potato.

---

4 heads of chicory, sliced widthways	2 garlic cloves, chopped	50ml double cream
50g butter	1 litre chicken, game or smoked ham stock	50g strong-flavoured cheese, such as mature Cheddar
2 leeks, finely sliced	1 bay leaf	Salt and ground white pepper
1 potato, diced	1 tbsp Dijon mustard	

If you want to curb the bitterness of the chicory, blanch it in the way outlined above.

Heat the butter in the base of the pressure cooker. When it is foaming, add the leeks, potato, garlic and the blanched or unblanched chicory. Stir for a couple of minutes over a high heat until everything starts to turn a golden colour. Add the stock and the bay leaf, then season with salt and white pepper. Close the lid and bring to high pressure. Cook for 2 minutes and release pressure naturally.

Check for doneness – everything should be very soft. Remove the bay leaf, then blitz the soup until smooth. Add the mustard, cream and cheese and stir until the cheese has melted.

Mushroom, Kale and Barley Soup

This very strong, cleansing, healthy soup is one for any garlic addict! If I have any leftover duck meat, I add some crisp shreds of it to this, right at the end. I might also add some cooked squash at the same time as the kale, for colour and sweetness. You can include dried mushrooms in this soup if you like. I would supplement the stock and the fresh mushrooms with between 10–20g of dried mushrooms. Soak, drain, reserving the liquid to add to the soup with the stock, then roughly chop and add to the soup at the same time as the barley.

3 tbsp olive oil
100g portobello mushrooms
2 heads of garlic, separated
  into cloves, half thinly sliced,
  half peeled and left whole

50g pearled barley, well rinsed
1 tbsp rice wine
750ml well-flavoured stock
Juice of ½ lemon

Large bunch of kale or other
  robust green, chopped
Salt and freshly ground pepper

Heat the olive oil in the pressure cooker and add the mushrooms and roughly three-quarters of the sliced garlic. Sauté gently for a while, making sure the garlic doesn't take on any colour, then add the barley. Stir, making sure the barley takes on a sheen from the oil, then pour over the rice wine. Allow to bubble furiously until it has almost evaporated. Add the stock and season well with salt and pepper. Throw in the whole garlic cloves, loosely tied in muslin if you prefer, for easy removal.

Close the lid and bring to high pressure. Cook for 18 minutes and fast release. Fish out the whole garlic cloves and reserve. Add the lemon juice, kale and the rest of the sliced garlic and close the lid again – cook for just 1 minute at high pressure and again fast release. Leave to simmer gently. Remove the flesh from the reserved garlic cloves and stir it back into the soup. This way you get a good combination of garlic – some bite and some mellow creaminess.

Borscht

My father loves all things Russian, including this soup, but he used to find the 3+ hours' cooking time a bit much. We spent one afternoon seeing if we could make borscht less of a daunting undertaking. We managed to cut the cooking time down and simplify his recipe to boot, and ended up with a clean, fresh-tasting soup with rich, meaty undertones. He's now a pressure cooker convert.

30g butter

600g beetroot, peeled, cut into quarters and thinly sliced

1 tbsp cider vinegar

3 tbsp oil or beef dripping

400g beef, cut into cubes

1 onion, chopped

A few dill sprigs (optional)

4 waxy potatoes, sliced

2 carrots, cut into rounds

½ white cabbage, roughly shredded

3 garlic cloves, finely chopped

3 tomatoes, peeled, seeded and finely chopped (or 150g tinned)

Salt and freshly ground pepper

Chopped flat-leaf parsley, to garnish

Soured cream, to serve

For the apple and horseradish relish (optional)

1 eating apple, peeled and coarsely grated

1 tsp freshly grated horseradish or 2 tsp hot horseradish sauce

1 tsp cider vinegar

If making the apple and horseradish relish, combine all the ingredients and season with salt and pepper. Store in a jar or plastic container in the fridge for up to a few days; it may start to brown, but this will not affect the flavour.

Heat half the butter in the base of the pressure cooker. Add the beetroot and the cider vinegar. Sauté for a couple of minutes then add 50ml water, close the lid, bring to high pressure and cook for 8 minutes. Release quickly and reserve the beetroot until later.

In the same pressure cooker, heat the oil or dripping over a medium–high heat. When it starts to smoke, add the beef and sear on all sides until browned. Add the onion and sauté for a couple of minutes longer. Season with a large pinch of salt and some black pepper. Pour in 1.5 litres of cold water. Bring to the boil and skim until any foam collecting on the top changes from brown to white. Add the dill, if using, then close the lid and bring to high pressure. Cook for 20 minutes and allow to release pressure naturally.

Meanwhile, prepare the rest of the vegetables. Towards the end of the beef's cooking time, heat a large frying pan and melt the remaining butter in it. Add the potatoes, carrots, cabbage and garlic and sauté gently for 5 minutes, adding the tomatoes for the final minute. Transfer all the vegetables to the pressure cooker, including the reserved beetroot, and check the seasoning. Close the lid and return to high pressure. Cook for 2 minutes and then fast release.

Serve with all or a combination of the chopped parsley, soured cream and apple and horseradish relish.

Starters, Snacks and Savouries

'I am a great believer in having something already made in the fridge, held in readiness for when you fancy a snack'

A fair few of the recipes in this chapter are of the prepare-ahead variety. That is because I am a great believer in having something already made in the fridge, held in readiness for when you fancy a snack, or made in anticipation of guests because you'd rather spend your time relaxing with them than rushing madly round the kitchen.

These kinds of dishes are also useful for lunches on the hoof – I work from home and if I'm not in the mood for soup, I will want something else ready-made that I can just pull from the fridge and eat with toast. But there's absolutely no reason why the same dishes shouldn't compose part of a lunchbox or picnic spread (in fact, Scotch eggs are made for this, the perfect portable food – see recipe on page 49).

I love leftovers and often deliberately make a large quantity of something so that I can use a portion of it for something else, so I give a few basic ideas here for things to do with leftovers from other dishes in this book. Eggs also feature heavily – you are never far away from a meal if you have eggs, and the pressure cooker helps you to make a couple of very elegant dishes very quickly indeed.

Eggs 'En Cocotte'

These are eggs baked in ramekins, often with some savoury morsel hidden underneath them and a covering of cream or cheese. This recipe uses mushrooms, but I have included a few other options in the variations below. These eggs normally take around 10 minutes in a pre-heated oven, so using the pressure cooker is a huge saving of time and fuel.

50g butter, plus more for greasing

100g mushrooms (I like portobellini)

1 large tarragon sprig, leaves only, chopped

2 garlic cloves, finely chopped

Squeeze of lemon juice

4 large eggs

4 tbsp double cream

Salt and freshly ground pepper

Strips of toast, to serve

Butter four ramekins and set aside. Put the upturned steamer basket in the pressure cooker and either put 3–4cm of water in the base and bring to the boil, or have a kettle of freshly boiled water handy for when you are ready to start cooking the eggs.

Heat the butter in a frying pan and, when it is foaming, add the mushrooms and chopped tarragon. Fry for 3–5 minutes until the mushrooms are dark and glossy and any juices have started to evaporate, then add the garlic and cook for a couple of minutes more. Season with salt and pepper, squeeze over the lemon juice, then divide between the ramekins. Break one egg into each ramekin, season again and top with a tablespoon of double cream.

Cover each ramekin tightly with a single layer of foil, then place on the upturned steamer basket in the cooker. Close the lid, bring to low pressure and cook for 4 minutes. Drop pressure quickly and serve straightaway with toast soldiers.

Variations

With asparagus spears

When asparagus is in season, the spears are perfect for dipping and – even better – can be cooked alongside the eggs. Trim, place on a sheet of foil, season with salt and pepper and drizzle with olive oil. Fold the foil around the asparagus to make a sealed parcel, then place on top of the ramekins in the pressure cooker. At low pressure, you should get perfect *al dente* asparagus.

With ham and cheese

Toss 75g chopped dry-cured ham with 1 teaspoon of finely chopped thyme and divide between four buttered ramekins. Add a tablespoon of double cream to each ramekin, break in an egg, season, and top with 50g grated Gruyère cheese. Cover and cook as before.

With tomatoes, peppers and saffron cream

Put 8 tablespoons of tomato sauce (see recipe on page 177), two skinned, chopped red peppers (see tip on page 182) and a pinch of hot paprika in a pan and heat up. When they are warmed through, stir in 2 teaspoons of sherry and allow to bubble furiously for a moment. Meanwhile warm through 4 tablespoons of double cream and add a pinch of saffron to it. Allow to infuse for a couple of minutes. Divide the tomato and pepper mixture between four ramekins, then pour over the saffron-infused cream. Break in the eggs, season, then top with 50g grated cheese – Cheddar is good. Cover and cook as before.

Parmesan Custards

The Parmesan custard offered in Rowley Leigh's West London restaurant, Le Café Anglais, is one of my all-time favourite dishes. The first time my husband and I tried it, we looked at one another and started laughing, so delighted were we with it. It has a rich flavour and silken texture – a little goes a long way, which is why these portions seem small until you actually start tucking in. I have experimented with different egg/liquid ratios and have found Rowley Leigh's version superior in every way, which is why I asked him if I could include it here. What I have changed is the accompanying toasts, which he makes with anchovy. As much as I love them, I wanted to try something slightly less salty (and therefore more child-friendly) so mine are made with shrimp. If you would prefer anchovy, simply crush six tinned anchovies with around 50g butter and use this mixture instead of the shrimp. If you can't find brown shrimp you can use a pot of potted shrimp instead.

Le Café Anglais serves these custards in tall china moulds, of only about 80ml capacity. I managed to find some large, handle-less espresso cups of similar dimensions, but you could use shallow ramekins without ill effect.

Butter, for greasing
50g finely grated Parmesan
150ml milk
150ml single cream
2 egg yolks
Pinch of cayenne pepper

Salt and freshly ground black
  and white pepper

For the shrimp toasts
100g cooked brown shrimp
50g butter, plus more for
  spreading

Squeeze of lemon juice
Grating of nutmeg
4 very thin slices of robust
  white sourdough bread

Cut out four circles of greaseproof paper, using the base circumference of your chosen receptacle as a template. Butter the paper circles and also your ramekins or cups.

Reserve 1 tablespoon of the Parmesan and put the rest into a heatproof bowl with the milk and cream. Place the bowl over a pan of boiling water and warm through, stirring occasionally, until the cheese has melted. Be patient, this will take longer than you would expect. Allow to cool completely, then whisk in the egg yolks, some salt and white pepper and the pinch of cayenne.

Divide the mixture between the ramekins and cover each with a buttered circle of greaseproof paper – it needs to be touching the custard, not sitting above it, but there is no need for any additional cover. Put the steamer basket, upturned, in your pressure cooker. Place the ramekins on top and carefully pour boiling water around them. Close the lid and bring to high pressure. Cook for 5 minutes for a very soft set (I favour this), or 6 minutes if you want it slightly firmer, then remove from the heat and release pressure quickly.

While the custards are cooking, make the toasts. Purée together the shrimp, butter, lemon juice, nutmeg, salt and black pepper in a blender or food processor. Spread this over half the slices of sourdough and cover with the remaining slices to make thin sandwiches. Butter the outsides of the bread and put in a heated sandwich maker, or grill on both sides in a frying pan. Cut into soldiers.

Sprinkle the remaining Parmesan over the custards and brown under a hot grill. Serve with the shrimp toasts.

Thai-spiced Crab Custards

This recipe was inspired by a Chinese recipe for savoury custards. However, I have used more Thai flavours in the infusion. The result is delicious – sweet, fragrant and light, especially if you allow the custards to rest for a few minutes after you remove them from the pressure cooker.

Butter, for greasing
Juice of 1 lime
100g white crab meat
150ml milk
150ml single cream
1 garlic clove, thinly sliced

2cm piece of root ginger, thinly sliced
1 lemongrass stalk, bruised
5cm strip of pared lime zest
2 kaffir lime leaves (optional)
1 tsp white peppercorns

4 eggs
½ tsp fish sauce
Salt and freshly ground white pepper

Butter four ramekins. Squeeze the lime juice over the crab meat and season well with salt and white pepper. Divide between the ramekins.

Put the milk and cream in a pan along with the garlic, ginger, lemongrass, lime zest, lime leaves (if using) and peppercorns. Slowly bring to the boil and immediately remove from the heat. Leave to infuse until cool.

Lightly beat the eggs in a bowl and pour over the infused milk and cream. Again lightly, stir so that everything is combined, then strain. Add the fish sauce. Divide the mixture between the ramekins and season with just a little salt.

Follow the same cooking instructions as for the Parmesan Custards on page 41, using greaseproof paper as described.

More Things to Eat with Toast

There are many recipes in this book that make perfect leftovers for quick lunches or snacks. Any of the bean dishes (see pages 122–30) will make superlative versions of beans on toast, especially if you melt some strong cheese on top. The Basque Squid Stew (see page 115) is good warmed through and piled onto sourdough, as are the two sardine recipes on pages 110–11. You can also pot sardines – simply purée, pile into ramekins or one larger dish and cover with clarified butter to preserve.

To make clarified butter, melt 100g butter very slowly in a pan. Remove from the heat when it begins to foam. Carefully spoon off all the foam and you will see that the butter has separated. Strain off the clear yellow liquid (this is your clarified butter) and discard the white residue left in the pan. For extra clarity, you can strain the clarified butter through muslin if you like.

Finally, try mashing up the Roasted Garlic on page 182 – good on its own, but even better with some crushed cherry tomatoes or roasted red pepper and roughly torn basil. Here are some other options:

Creamed Courgettes with Brown Shrimp

Very unfashionable this, but I love courgettes cooked very slowly in butter to the point that they start breaking down into a melting creaminess.

50g butter, plus more to serve	50g brown shrimp	Salt and freshly ground pepper
1 tbsp olive oil	Handful of basil, roughly torn	Toasted sourdough bread, to serve
2 large courgettes, thinly sliced on the diagonal	Grating of nutmeg	
	Squeeze of lemon juice	

Melt the butter and oil in the bottom of the pressure cooker. Add the courgettes and stir for a couple of minutes until the courgettes are glossy with butter. Season with salt and pepper. Close the lid and bring to high pressure. Remove from the heat immediately and allow to drop pressure naturally – this will not take long. Return to a low heat and allow any liquid to evaporate.

Throw in the brown shrimp and basil and gently turn over until all is combined. Grate over a dusting of nutmeg and squeeze over some lemon juice. Pile onto toasted sourdough bread spread liberally with butter.

Rillettes

Rillettes are an excellent way of using up tough cuts of meat or bits (such as small legs on game birds) that are often discarded or left for the stockpot. You can use many kinds of meat, especially game, poultry and pork. Rabbit is also popular, but not with me – I am not keen on the texture. A frugal version can be made using game or poultry carcasses along with belly pork – you get a very good flavour this way, while still being able to save most of the meat for other things. If you decide to take this route, increase the amount of belly pork by 250g and try to take as much meat from the carcasses as possible once they have been cooked.

50g butter or dripping

250g meat – I like duck
   or game legs, or pork
   shoulder (or the carcasses
   described above)

500g belly pork,
   cut into 2cm cubes

½ tsp salt

½ tsp crushed
   white peppercorns

1 tsp allspice berries
   or juniper berries

1 mace blade

2 bay leaves

2 garlic cloves, finely chopped

A few curly parsley sprigs

150ml white wine

Heat the butter in the pressure cooker and add all the meat. Fry over a very low heat until everything is a light golden brown. Try to do this quite slowly as you want the belly pork to start releasing fat (this is called 'rendering'). Drain off all the fat and reserve.

Add all the other ingredients to the cooker, then close the lid and bring to high pressure. Cook for 30 minutes and allow to drop pressure naturally. The meat should be extremely soft and tender. Drain the meat and reserve the cooking liquor. When it is cool enough to handle, shred all the meat, discarding any bone, fat and skin as you go and picking out the herbs and spices.

At this point you have a choice – you can leave the meat as it is, just finely shredded, or you can process it until smooth. Check the meat for seasoning and add more salt, pepper or spices as you like. Put into ramekins or an earthenware pot. Reduce the cooking liquid by half and add the reserved fat to it. Pour the liquid over the meat in the ramekins to just cover. This will act as a preservative. The rillettes should keep in the fridge for a week.

More Dips and Spreads

Hummus

If you are making any other chickpea dish, cook double the amount of chickpeas so you have some leftover for hummus. You might want to cook them for a little longer to get them softer, or soak them first, adding a good pinch of bicarbonate of soda. The following quantities are for around 250g cooked chickpeas. Mix 1–2 tablespoons of tahini with the juice of 1–2 lemons (start with one of each and build up, depending on taste). Purée the chickpeas with a little of their cooking water, add two crushed garlic cloves, ½ teaspoon of ground cumin and 1 teaspoon of salt, then add the tahini and lemon mixture and purée again. Put into a dish, sprinkle with cayenne pepper and cover with a glug of good olive oil.

Baba Ganoush

The ingredients for baba ganoush are very similar to those of hummus. Instead of chickpeas, use roasted aubergines (see method on page 182), making sure that you char the skins as much as possible. Scrape out all the softened flesh, add to it the same ingredients as for the hummus recipe and cover with olive oil.

Bean Purées

You can make purées with any number of beans. I like to use cannellini beans – I add rosemary to the cooking water, then roasted garlic, chilli and parsley to the purée. Some dried mint is also good, as is a generous sprinkling of sumac.

Scotch Eggs

It may seem odd to include a recipe for Scotch eggs in a pressure cooker book – they're deep-fried of course, and you cannot under any circumstances deep-fry in a pressure cooker! However, I discovered that if you steam eggs on a low pressure for 3–4 minutes (depending on size), not only will you end up with ridiculously easy-to-peel eggs, but you will also have a mollet egg – an egg with a runny yolk and a just-set white. This means that even the clumsiest of us have a good chance of being able to make a Scotch egg with a soft centre.

The hardest part was finding something on which to balance the eggs, to stop them rattling around the steamer basket. Fortunately, I came across the excellent idea of using upturned olive oil or wine bottle caps – you can balance an egg on them perfectly.

There are many variations on the Scotch egg these days – they can be made with black pudding or venison, vegetarian with beans, chickpeas, or cheese with mashed potatoes, but I've stuck to a classic pork sausagemeat here. I've also suggested a smoked haddock variation (pictured), inspired by the flavours of kedgeree, which has a very light, delicate flavour – add the cheese for something richer. Finally, there is *Nargisi Kofta* – a traditional Indian dish, which, according to unconfirmed rumours, was the inspiration for the original Scotch egg. It is very popular with my husband's family, who all adore eggs. I give you a sauceless version, but try eating it with a raita of yoghurt, mint and cucumber.

---

4 large eggs, plus 2 medium eggs, beaten
Plain flour, for dusting
100g fine breadcrumbs
Vegetable or groundnut oil, for deep-frying

For a traditional pork casing:
220g sausagemeat or skinned sausages
Zest of one lemon or lime
1 tsp thyme leaves

1 tbsp dried sage
½ small onion, very finely chopped

First cook the four large eggs. It's a good idea to have a bowl of very cold or iced water ready, to drop the eggs into once they've been steamed. Put around 5cm water in the base of the pressure cooker, then add the trivet and the steamer. Balance your eggs, pointy-end down, on upturned bottle caps. Close the lid, bring to low pressure and cook for 3½–4 minutes depending on the size of your egg, then release immediately. Plunge the eggs into the cold water and leave until they are cool enough to handle, then gently break the shells and peel off. Return the peeled eggs to the cold water.

To make the pork casing, mix together the sausagemeat with the onion, zest and herbs. Divide into four portions (I weigh it). Dust your hands with flour and flatten each piece, either by hand, or by rolling between pieces of cling film. Gently dry the eggs and lightly dust with flour, then mould each flattened piece of filling around each egg. Dip each coated egg into the beaten egg, then the breadcrumbs.

If you have a deep-fat fryer, add vegetable or groundnut oil and heat it to 180°C. Otherwise, heat the oil in a deep, heavy-based pan, being careful not to overfill it and either use a thermometer or test the heat with a piece of bread – it should turn golden within 30 seconds. Fry the eggs until golden brown, usually between 3–5 minutes. Drain on kitchen paper and cool. Serve the eggs split in two, ideally at a picnic.

Variations

For a kedgeree-inspired casing

Put 220g white and smoked haddock – as dry as possible – into a food processor with a chopped small onion or shallot, a roughly chopped 2cm piece of root ginger, a garlic clove, 1 teaspoon of mild curry powder, 1 tablespoon of chopped parsley or coriander leaf and 50g strong cheese (optional). Lightly season, using salt and white peppercorns if possible. This is a delicate filling, so could do with some chilling before you try and mould it round your eggs. I flatten it out on cling film and put it in the fridge for a short time. Then complete the recipe as before.

For the *Nargisi Kofta* casing

In a food processor, put 220g finely minced lamb, ½ a finely grated onion, a chopped garlic clove, a grated 2cm piece of root ginger, ¼ teaspoon each of ground cloves, cinnamon and turmeric, ½ teaspoon each of cayenne pepper, ground cumin, salt and ground black pepper, a grating of nutmeg and 1 tablespoon of chopped coriander leaf. Whiz until everything is blended and the meat is very fine. Mix in 1 tablespoon of thick plain yoghurt and chill for a while to firm up. Then complete the recipe as before.

Pulled Meat Sandwiches

Pulled meat is one of the best things to have in the fridge, ready for a midday sandwich or snack. A speciality of the American Deep South, it normally takes a minimum of 7 hours' smoking, rather than the 45–60 minutes achievable in the pressure cooker. The meat (usually pork shoulder, which the Americans call 'butt', or brisket if you prefer beef) is coated in a spice rub then slowly smoked, before being shredded and served with barbecue sauce in a bun, with lots of garnishes, such as coleslaw, melted cheese, or a punchy salsa.

For my recipe I decided against using a rub and instead put all the flavours into a cooking sauce. Chipotle (smoked jalapeño) and Liquid Smoke (a common US ingredient, sold by some online UK stockists) give all the smokiness you need. This doesn't have a hard-hitting chilli flavour, it's more a slowly encroaching warmth. If you want more heat, add either more chipotle or some cayenne pepper to the paste, and feel free to add chilli to the salsa.

1 tbsp vegetable oil	**For the paste**	**For the salsa**
1.5kg pork shoulder or beef brisket (I have also used pig cheeks or beef shin)	1 medium onion, finely chopped	6 tomatillos or tomatoes, seeded and finely chopped
200g tin of chopped tomatoes	4 garlic cloves, chopped	1 red onion, finely chopped
100ml beer or water	1 dried chipotle, roughly chopped, or 1 tbsp dried chipotle powder	Small bunch of coriander, leaves only, finely chopped
¼ tsp Liquid Smoke (see above)	1 tbsp soft light brown sugar	Juice of 1 lime
Salt	1 tbsp cider vinegar	1 tsp sherry vinegar (optional)
	1 tsp dried oregano	½ tsp sugar
	2 tsp ground cumin	Salt and freshly ground pepper
	1 tsp white pepper	
	¼ tsp ground cinnamon	

First make the salsa. Combine all the ingredients together and allow to stand so that the flavours have a chance to meld. This will keep for a couple of days in the fridge but is best served at room temperature.

Put all the paste ingredients into a food processor and blitz until fairly smooth. If you find that they are sticking a little, add some water until they mix together properly.

Put the oil in the pressure cooker over a medium heat. Add the meat and brown thoroughly on all sides, allowing it to release as much fat as possible. Remove the meat from the cooker and set aside. Add the paste to the cooker, fry for a couple of minutes, then add the tomatoes, beer or water and the Liquid Smoke, and season with salt.

Return the meat to the cooker, close the lid and bring to high pressure. The cooking time depends on the cut of meat you are using. If you are using pig cheeks, cook for 30 minutes. For a large piece of brisket or pork shoulder, cook for a full hour. Remove the pressure cooker from the heat and allow to release pressure naturally.

Remove the meat and simmer the remaining liquid in the cooker for a minute or two, but do not let it reduce too much – it needs to be wet but not too watery. Taste – if you think it needs more Liquid Smoke, add it now, but be sparing, as even very little can overwhelm the other flavours. While the sauce is simmering, shred the meat with two forks, removing any pieces of fat. Return the meat to the sauce and combine. It is now ready to serve with the salsa, or can be stored in the fridge and reheated any time you fancy a sandwich. I do this by frying it quickly in a frying pan until some of the meat shreds brown and crisp up a little.

Beef and Beetroot Jelly with Horseradish Cream

If you are the sort of person who loves the savoury jelly found in pork pies or on the base of a cooling roast chicken, you will love this recipe. It's an old-fashioned dish of cooked meat suspended in a clear, savoury jelly – a kind of beefy cousin to the porcine brawn and a less-elegant precursor to the aspic jellies currently offered by some restaurants. It is also a very adaptable recipe – you could simply use a well-flavoured reduced chicken stock with some poached chicken, or even turn it into the dish that my mother-in-law calls 'paya', which uses goat or mutton and is spiced with chilli and masala spices. Or you can try adding cooked, diced vegetables or herbs to the jelly. Make sure that whichever kind of meat you use, it is a gelatinous cut – you need it to be able to set.

Don't make the horseradish cream too hot or it will really interfere with the flavour of the jelly, so be sparing with the horseradish. If you can't find fresh, use a hot horseradish sauce instead, but not a creamed version.

200g ox cheeks, shin of beef or similar	1 bay leaf	**For the horseradish cream**
750ml cold beef stock or water	1 large parsley sprig	200ml crème fraîche
1 onion, thickly sliced	1 mace blade	1cm piece of horseradish, peeled and finely grated, or 1 tbsp hot horseradish sauce
2 carrots, cut into quarters	2 cloves	
1 celery stick, cut into large chunks	1 tsp black peppercorns, lightly crushed	1 tsp cider vinegar (if you are using fresh horseradish)
2 beetroot, cut into cubes	1 tbsp port (optional)	Pinch of sea salt
3 garlic cloves, chopped	Oil, for greasing	
	Salt and freshly ground pepper	

To make the horseradish cream, mix together all the ingredients, then put in the fridge to chill.

Put the meat in the pressure cooker and pour over cold stock or water until it is just covered. Bring to the boil and skim off any scum that rises to the top, until it turns from a gritty mushroom-brown to a clean white. Add all the vegetables, herbs and spices. Season with salt. Close the lid, bring to high pressure and cook for 30 minutes. Allow to release pressure naturally.

Strain the contents of the pressure cooker through a sieve, then line the sieve with (preferably) muslin or a thin-weave tea towel, or kitchen roll at a pinch, and strain the liquid again. You now have two choices: you can either try to skim off most of the fat and reduce the liquid now, or you can wait until the fat has set for easier removal and then reduce it. I usually do the latter, as it generally results in a clearer jelly. However, if you were meticulous with your straining you should be okay to continue immediately. Put the liquid in a pan and boil fiercely to reduce by about one-third – you need around 500ml liquid. Towards the end, add the port, if using, then check for seasoning and add more salt accordingly. Meanwhile, shred the ox cheeks, removing any sticky, gelatinous bits that may remain.

Grease a bowl or terrine dish lightly with oil (or the jelly is also very pretty when turned out from individual moulds). Pour over some of the liquid and put in the fridge for 15–20 minutes until it has set enough that the ox cheeks won't settle right into it. Spread over the ox cheeks then pour over the rest of the liquid and gently stir to get an even distribution of meat. Chill in the fridge, stirring every 5 minutes to start with, to make sure the beef isn't floating to the top. When the jelly has set (which takes a few hours), scrape off any fat – this is worth saving for use in cooking (especially for frying potatoes). Serve with quenelles of the horseradish cream.

Meat

'The miracle of the pressure cooker is that you can achieve the same results in normally less than 30 minutes, rather than it taking over 2 hours'

One of the best things to happen in food in the past few years is the rediscovery of cuts of meat that were all but forgotten. I'm thinking of tough, hardworking cuts such as cheeks, which ordinarily need very careful handling – long, slow cooking, just below simmering point – to become tender rather than something resembling old leather. The miracle of the pressure cooker is that you can achieve the same results in less than 30 minutes, rather than it taking over 2 hours.

There are still a few rules to follow. For really tender meat, it is always advisable to let the pressure drop naturally. You will then normally need to reduce the cooking liquor a little. Please let it cool down and rest for a while before you start tasting it. Just like anything cooked conventionally, most meaty stews and curries are best left a day and reheated. Not only can you skim off any fat very effectively that way because it will have set, but the flavours will also have developed further. It has been suggested to me that this is defeating the object of cooking with a pressure cooker – the whole point being its immediacy. I disagree. You are saving a huge amount of time and fuel on the cooking, and you can make things for the next day quickly in the evening, without having to stay up until they've finished cooking. Of course, you do not have to obey my overnight rule; in an emergency I have made a casserole with frozen meat and served it half an hour later – it will still be tender and taste good, just not quite as good as it would the following day.

I have concentrated on braises and casseroles in this chapter, but there are a couple of other ways to cook meat in the pressure cooker that are useful to know. You can 'poach' meat in the pressure cooker very quickly by completely covering in liquid, the advantages being that you can add whatever aromatics you like to give flavour and that you will have a flavoured broth to use as stock. An ideal cut for this is brisket, which takes around 45–50 minutes for a 1–1.5kg piece.

You can also steam the meat. I have cooked roasting joints of beef and pork this way and seared them afterwards in a hot frying pan. The meat stays very moist and the fat gets 'steam treated' – similar to pouring endless kettles of boiling water over a duck before you roast it – so should crisp up nicely for crackling. A 1kg piece should take around 25 minutes; a 500g piece, half that.

Any casserole, stew or curry can be adapted for the pressure cooker. Just remember to reduce the amount of liquid, as much less will be lost during the cooking period, and reduce the cooking time by around two-thirds. Any vegetables that you want to be edible (i.e., not simply there to add flavour to the sauce) should be added towards the end of the cooking time. If you have time, allow to release pressure naturally then add the vegetables and continue to cook.

Ragù

I make quite a lot of this at once and freeze it. It's very useful to have portioned up, as it can be used for so many things – pasta (spaghetti or lasagne), in cottage or shepherd's pie, or for moussaka, if made from lamb. Sometimes I add chicken livers as well, or, to bulk it out and add creaminess, some cooked brown lentils. Don't forget that you can use pretty much any kind of meat here – lamb, veal, pork, venison, and vary the flavours and type of alcohol used accordingly.

1–2 tbsp olive oil

1kg good-quality minced beef, lamb or other meat

1 large onion, finely chopped

2 large carrots, finely diced

2 celery sticks, finely diced

4 garlic cloves, finely chopped

1 thyme sprig

1 tbsp very finely chopped rosemary

2 bay leaves

Generous pinch of ground cinnamon

½ bottle of red wine

400g tin of chopped tomatoes

1 tbsp tomato ketchup

Salt and freshly ground pepper

Heat 1 tablespoon of olive oil in the pressure cooker and quickly brown the meat. You will probably have to do this in batches. Remove the meat from the cooker.

Add more oil if necessary, then fry the onion, carrots and celery, also quite quickly so that they take on colour. Add the garlic, herbs and the cinnamon, then return the meat to the pan. Keep the heat fairly high and pour in the wine a glass at a time, allowing the sauce to reduce by at least half after each addition. Add the tomatoes and ketchup and season well with salt and pepper.

Close the lid and bring to high pressure. Cook for 15 minutes then release pressure naturally. Leave to simmer and reduce for at least another 10 minutes if you can. Fish out the thyme stalk and bay leaves before serving.

Variation

Chilli

Follow the ragù recipe, adding a finely diced red pepper with the onion and celery and omitting the carrot. Replace the rosemary with dried oregano, and when you add the cinnamon, add also 1 tablespoon of ground cumin, 1 teaspoon of ground allspice and as much chilli as you like (I use a combination of cayenne pepper and some dried chipotle or chipotle en adobo for smokiness). When you have cooked it, stir in 200g cooked beans (I prefer black beans to red kidney beans) and around 25g dark chocolate. Simmer until the chocolate has melted and the sauce has reduced down.

Beef Braised in Red Wine, Orange Zest and Tarragon

This is my basic recipe for a beef casserole, which can be varied endlessly: you can change the cooking liquid and the aromatics, turning it from a classic red wine braise to a more English beef cooked in stout, or even use smaller dice of beef to make a chilli that is more authentic than the mince version. A note on the type of meat here: I prefer to use ox cheeks – they're cheap, full of flavour and stay very moist when they are cooked.

Vegetable oil or lard, for cooking

1.5kg ox cheek, beef flank or shin, cut into 8–10cm pieces

Plain flour, for dusting

2 carrots, roughly chopped

1 celery stick, roughly chopped

1 onion, roughly chopped

2 tbsp brandy (optional)

½ bottle of red wine

1 head of garlic, separated into unpeeled cloves

5cm strip of pared orange zest

Small bunch of tarragon

1 thyme sprig

1 bay leaf

Salt and freshly ground pepper

Mashed potatoes or dumplings, to serve

Heat a shallow layer of vegetable oil or lard in the base of the pressure cooker. Dust your meat with flour and shake off the excess. Sear the meat until browned on all sides – you may have to do this in batches. Remove the meat from the pressure cooker.

Add a little more oil if necessary and throw in the carrots, celery and onion. Fry over a high heat until they are starting to caramelise. Add the brandy, if using, and use it to deglaze the pressure cooker, allowing it to bubble up while you scrape off any bits stuck on the bottom of the cooker. If you don't have any brandy to hand, use a little of the red wine instead. Return the meat to the pressure cooker along with the garlic, orange zest and herbs, which you should spread evenly over the meat. Pour over the red wine and season with salt and pepper.

Close the lid and bring to high pressure, then cook for 25 minutes. Remove from the heat and allow the pressure to drop naturally. Remove the meat from the pressure cooker, then strain the rest of the contents through a sieve. Discard the vegetables and aromatics and return the liquid to the pressure cooker. Simmer over a medium heat until the cooking liquor has reduced slightly and the flavours have concentrated into a sauce. Return the meat to the cooker and gently warm through. Serve with mashed potatoes or dumplings. (For a more substantial one-pot dish, take a selection of vegetables (potatoes, celery, carrots, etc.), cut into large pieces and add to the reduced cooking liquid before the meat is added back in. Cook for another 3 minutes at high pressure, fast release, then return the meat to the cooker and warm it through.)

Keema Peas

You could describe this as an Indian version of ragù – it's a mild, sweet and aromatic way of currying ground lamb or mutton and is especially good with flatbreads such as naan or chapati. For something more substantial, when you don't want to cook rice and don't have any flatbreads, add some waxy potatoes just before cooking at high pressure. Don't be worried about the long list of spices – it's just a case of assembling them. Or if you don't have them, substitute with 1½ tablespoons of your favourite curry powder.

2 tbsp vegetable oil or ghee
1 onion, very finely chopped
2 garlic cloves, finely chopped
2cm piece of root ginger, grated
500g minced lamb
Small bunch of coriander, leaves and stems separated
½ tsp turmeric

Pinch of cayenne pepper
1 cinnamon stick
2 cloves
2 black cardamom pods
4 green cardamom pods
1 tsp coriander seed
1 tsp cumin seed
1 tsp black peppercorns

1 bay leaf
1 tomato, seeded and finely chopped
250g fresh or frozen peas
2 spring onions, shredded
2 mild green chillies, seeded and finely shredded
Squeeze of lemon juice
Salt

Heat the oil in the pressure cooker and fry the onion, garlic and ginger. Add the lamb mince, along with the chopped coriander stems, turmeric and cayenne pepper and stir over a medium heat until the mince is well browned.

Put all the whole spices and the bay leaf in a piece of muslin and secure. Add the bag of spices to the cooker along with the tomato and cook for 1 minute. Pour in 100ml water, season with salt (around ½ teaspoon) and tip in the peas. Close the lid and bring to high pressure. Cook for 15 minutes. Release pressure quickly and put onto a low heat.

Add the spring onions, green chillies, lemon juice and coriander leaves and allow to simmer for a couple of minutes or so before serving.

Pork Osso Buco

This dish is usually made with veal shanks that have been cut across the bone, but the pork equivalent is a fraction of the price and, in my opinion, much tastier. Feel free to use veal if you prefer. I have also seen a venison version, which is much richer and uses exactly the same ingredients. The traditional accompaniment is Risotto alla Milanese (see recipe on page 150). You can make the osso buco first (even the day before) and transfer to a casserole dish or pan, freeing up your pressure cooker for the risotto. However, please do not stir the gremolata into the sauce until just before you are ready to serve.

4 osso buco shanks (see above)
1 tbsp plain flour
2 tbsp olive oil
25g butter
1 onion, finely chopped
1 large carrot, finely diced
1 celery stick, finely chopped
4 garlic cloves, finely chopped

150ml white wine
100ml chicken or meat stock
150g tinned chopped tomatoes
   or 3 fresh tomatoes, peeled,
   seeded and chopped
Bouquet garni (see page 16) of
   2 bay leaves, sage and
   flat-leaf parsley
Salt and freshly ground pepper

Risotto alla Milanese,
   to serve (optional)

For the gremolata
Grated zest of 1 lemon
1 garlic clove
1 tbsp chopped
   flat-leaf parsley

Dust the osso buco shanks with flour. Heat the olive oil and butter in the pressure cooker. Sauté the onion, carrot and celery until they have started to take on some colour, then add the garlic for the final minute. Remove from the pressure cooker, turn up the heat and add the meat. Fry until all sides have a good colour. Pour in the wine and allow it to simmer until it has almost completely evaporated.

Return the vegetables to the cooker along with the stock, tomatoes and bouquet garni. Season with salt and pepper. Close the lid, bring to high pressure and cook for 20 minutes. Allow to drop pressure naturally.

While the osso buco is cooking, make the gremolata. Simply chop everything finely and mix together.

Remove the meat from the pressure cooker and strain everything else through a sieve, pushing the soft vegetables through. Simmer the sauce to reduce a little if necessary and return the meat to the pressure cooker. Sprinkle over half the gremolata and allow to meld with the other flavours for a couple of minutes over a low heat. Serve with the remaining gremolata to pass around and the risotto, if you like.

Pig Cheeks Marinated in Red Wine and Rosemary

Pig cheeks are probably the cheapest of all cheap cuts available, which I find incredible considering that they are also one of the best tasting. Not only that, thanks to all the connective tissue, they have a texture that is moist with an unctuous stickiness – very hard to resist! Pig cheeks can handle strong, robust flavours and their sweetness tempers the punchiness of the red wine and rosemary in this particular dish. For a completely different taste, consider substituting the wine with cider and use juniper and sage instead of the rosemary, thyme and tarragon.

12 pig cheeks

1 large rosemary sprig, roughly chopped

3 fat garlic cloves, sliced

1 tsp black peppercorns, very coarsely ground

½ bottle of robust red wine

1 tbsp olive oil

25g butter

2 carrots, finely diced

1 large onion, finely chopped

1 celery stick, finely diced

1 thyme sprig

1 tarragon sprig

Salt

Creamy mashed potato, to serve

Put the pig cheeks in a non-metallic container and rub with the rosemary, garlic and peppercorns. Pour over the red wine and put in the refrigerator to marinate for as long as possible, preferably overnight.

Heat the oil and butter in the pressure cooker. Take the pig cheeks from the marinade (reserving the marinade for later) and pat dry. Sear in the cooker until brown, then remove. Add the carrots, onion and celery and sauté over a fairly high heat until they start to caramelise. Return the pig cheeks to the cooker, add the thyme and tarragon, then pour over the reserved marinade. Add a pinch of salt to season. Lock down the lid and bring the cooker to high pressure. Cook for 20 minutes then allow to drop pressure naturally.

Remove the pig cheeks from the cooker and fish out the sprig of thyme if it is particularly woody. Blitz the liquor with a hand blender until fairly smooth, then pass through a sieve. Return the liquid to the pressure cooker or a pan and boil rapidly to reduce until it is a deep brown and the consistency of a good gravy. Return the pig cheeks to the sauce and gently reheat before serving with creamy mashed potato.

Chinese Spare Ribs

I used to frequent a Chinese restaurant that made these, and it was the one dish on their menu that I could never forgo. The chef wouldn't give me a definitive recipe, so I have endured much trial and error in trying to recreate it. The one thing he did tell me was that the ribs are simmered for 7 hours. The pressure cooker cuts this down to 30 minutes. In fact, to cook ribs until tender only takes about 15 minutes in the pressure cooker, but to do this dish justice, you need to cook them for longer, until the bones themselves seem soft enough to eat and the meat is yielding and unctuous. An added bonus is the sauce – if you have any left over, it keeps for a while in the fridge (a layer of fat will form on top and act as preservative) and works very well as a dipping sauce.

2 tbsp vegetable oil

1kg meaty pork spare ribs, cut in half if possible

6 garlic cloves, crushed

5cm piece of root ginger, grated

5–6cm piece of cinnamon stick

½ star anise

1 tsp Szechuan pepper

1 red chilli, left whole

150ml soy sauce

100ml rice or cider vinegar

200ml apple juice

75g soft light brown sugar

½ bunch spring onions

Salt and freshly ground pepper

Heat the oil in the pressure cooker. Add the ribs and fry until nicely browned. You may have to do this in two batches. Add the garlic, ginger, cinnamon, star anise and Szechuan pepper and fry for a moment or two. Pierce the chilli a few times with the point of a small knife and add that too. Pour over the soy sauce, vinegar and apple juice, sprinkle in the sugar, then season with salt and pepper. Close the lid, bring up to high pressure and cook for 30 minutes. Remove from the heat and allow the pressure to drop naturally.

Remove the ribs and the chilli from the pressure cooker and return it to the heat. Simmer the liquid until it has reduced to a fairly light syrup. Return the ribs to the cooker and, if you are serving immediately, heat through again. But if you can, wait until the following day as the flavours will improve overnight.

To serve, trim the spring onions, cut in half widthways, and finely shred lengthways. Sprinkle over the ribs.

Hocks and Other Cuts of Ham

Ham hocks, gammon or bacon joints – whichever cut of smoked or unsmoked, cured pork you prefer to use – all work brilliantly in the pressure cooker and are extremely useful. So useful, in fact, that I often cook them for general use, rather than for a specific meal. They can be used in pasta sauces, risottos and soups, added to pots of beans for extra flavour, included in a creamy chicken pie or, best of all, simply eaten in a sandwich with copious amounts of mustard. The other wondrous thing about cooking a ham is that you end up with a delicious stock, which marries brilliantly with so many things, particularly beans, peas and lentils. Try using it in the Caribbean Smoked Ham and Red Lentil Soup on page 30.

Most hams require soaking in cold water overnight before you cook them. The alternative is to put in a pan of cold water, bring to the boil and immediately drain. Discard the water and proceed as below. You can then vary what you cook your ham in. Here I have added cider to the water, or you could also substitute beer. I have even made the US Deep South's trashy Coca Cola version, although I found the resulting liquor a bit sweet for use in all but the most savoury of soups, and the ham much drier and denser in texture than usual. I also substitute all kinds of aromatics for those given here.

The instructions below refer to cooking a couple of small ham hocks. If you want to cook a larger joint (for example, if you wanted a glazed Christmas ham), the rule of thumb is to cook at high pressure for 10 minutes per 500g of meat.

---

2 small ham hocks
(or 1 large, see above)
250ml cider
½ onion, kept in one piece

2 cloves
2 bay leaves
½ tsp allspice berries, lightly
crushed (optional)

1 tsp black peppercorns
1 rosemary sprig

Soak your ham hocks in cold water overnight or pre-boil as described above. Put your hams in the pressure cooker and cover with the cider, or your liquid of choice, then top up with water until the ham is covered. Bring to the boil and skim off all the foam. Add all the other ingredients. Close the lid and bring to high pressure. Cook for 30 minutes (possibly longer if cooking a large joint, see above), then allow to release naturally.

Remove the ham from the pressure cooker. When cool enough to handle, remove the skin. Your ham is now ready to use. Strain the cooking liquor and reserve for future use.

Ham Hocks with Braised Vegetables and Mustard Cream Sauce

I like the combination of apple and celeriac in this dish, but feel free to vary the vegetables if you want. It's good with wedges of cabbage and even a handful or two of peas. Here I have chosen a light mustard sauce, but at other times I serve this with a béchamel sauce made with some of the cooking liquor and milk, then flavoured with finely ground white pepper or finely chopped parsley.

1–2 ham hocks, cooked as described on page 69

100ml reserved cooking liquor

Around 300g new potatoes, halved

3 large carrots, cut into large chunks

2 celery sticks, cut widthways into large pieces

1 piece of celeriac, cut into large cubes

2 leeks, cut into 4cm lengths

1 head of garlic, separated into unpeeled cloves

1 tbsp olive oil

1 small eating apple, peeled and sliced into thin wedges

1 tbsp finely chopped curly parsley

Salt and freshly ground pepper

For the sauce

150ml reserved cooking liquor

½ tsp dried sage or 1 tsp chopped fresh

150ml double cream

1 tbsp Dijon mustard, plus more to serve

Cook the ham hocks as described on page 69, then pull the meat into large pieces. Put the reserved cooking liquor into the pressure cooker and add all the vegetables. Wrap the garlic and olive oil in a foil parcel (as described on page 182) and place on top of the vegetables. Close the lid and bring to high pressure. Cook for 4 minutes, then fast release.

Remove the garlic parcel from the pressure cooker, then add the ham pieces to the vegetables, along with the apple. Check for seasoning, adding salt and pepper as needed. Make sure you taste first, as ham hocks are already salty. Keep on a very low simmer to allow the meat to warm through and the apple to cook.

Meanwhile, make the sauce. Put the cooking liquor into a pan with the dried sage and reduce until you have just a couple of tablespoons left. Add the cream and keep simmering until the sauce has started to reduce and thicken. Take the garlic out of its foil parcel, remove the skin and mash the flesh, also removing any green cores. Add this to the sauce along with the mustard. Check for seasoning and allow to simmer for a minute or two longer, so that the flavours have a chance to combine.

Ladle the meat and vegetables into shallow bowls and pour over the sauce, where it should bleed into the other cooking juices. Sprinkle with the chopped parsley and serve with extra mustard on the side, if you like. (See photograph on page 68.)

Braised Lamb and Aubergines

I love all the flavours of moussaka, but sometimes want something less substantial, and this dish fits the bill perfectly. The first time I made it, I was in Greece and used a local wine that was very light, particularly when compared to the robust reds we are used to at home. I think it transformed the dish, so if you can find something similarly light, please try it. Adding anchovies to meat dishes is a favourite trick of mine, as it adds a savoury depth of flavour, but it isn't essential.

4 tbsp olive oil

1kg lamb (shoulder or neck fillet), cut into 5cm cubes

1 small onion, chopped

3 garlic cloves, finely chopped

½ tsp ground cinnamon

2 tsp cumin seed, roughly crushed

1 tsp dried oregano

4 anchovies, finely chopped (optional)

150ml light-bodied red wine

200g tinned chopped tomatoes

2 large aubergines, cut into large dice

Handful of black olives, pitted

Salt and freshly ground pepper

Chopped flat-leaf parsley or mint, to garnish

Put the olive oil in the pressure cooker and heat until it is very hot. Add the lamb and onion, and fry until both are nicely browned. Add the garlic, cinnamon, cumin and oregano, and the anchovies if you are using them, and cook for a minute or two, then pour in the red wine. Season with salt and pepper.

Close the lid and bring to high pressure, then cook for 20 minutes. Allow to drop pressure naturally. When you can safely remove the lid, add the tomatoes and aubergines, then replace the lid and cook for a further 3 minutes. Again, allow to drop pressure naturally. Return to the heat and stir for a minute or two, then cook until everything is well amalgamated and the liquid has started to reduce. Add the olives at this point so that they start to absorb some of the flavours. When you are ready to serve, sprinkle with chopped mint or parsley.

To turn into a more substantial one-pot meal

Add 500g new potatoes, cut in half lengthways, along with the tomatoes and aubergines. They should cook in the same time as the aubergine and will definitely be ready by the time you have reduced the sauce down a little.

Peruvian Lamb Stew *(Seco de Carnero)*

This Peruvian lamb stew was an absolute revelation for me when I first tried it. It happens to incorporate some of my favourite flavours, but I couldn't imagine how they would work together. But they do, so well. Sour orange juice and a paste of fresh green coriander, chilli and garlic create a hot and sour combination that cuts through the fatty lamb and is eventually tempered by sweet-tasting potatoes and peas. The potatoes and peas are best cooked on the day you are going to serve the dish, so if you are making it ahead, remember to wait before adding them.

50g fresh coriander, chopped, plus more to garnish

1–3 hot red chillies (quantity according to taste), seeded

½ head of garlic, separated into cloves and peeled

2 tbsp olive oil

Large knob of butter

1 medium onion, finely chopped

1kg lamb or mutton shoulder, cut into large pieces

250ml sour orange juice (Seville) or ⅔ orange juice with ⅓ lime juice

1kg new or waxy potatoes, cut into thick slices

500g fresh or frozen peas

Salt and freshly ground pepper

Make a fairly smooth paste from the coriander, chillies, garlic and 1 tablespoon of the olive oil. This is most easily done in a food processor or using a hand blender attachment.

Put the other tablespoon of olive oil and the butter in the pressure cooker. Heat until the butter has melted and started to froth around the edges, then add the onion. Sauté until the onion is soft, then add the paste. Cook for a minute or two longer, stirring all the while, then add the meat. Cook for several minutes, turning regularly until the pieces are starting to go brown and are covered in the sauce. Season with salt and pepper.

Pour in the citrus juice and close the lid. Bring to high pressure and cook for 25 minutes. Allow to drop pressure naturally. The liquid should be quite syrupy and the meat should be very tender. If you feel that the liquid could be slightly thicker, reduce by simmering for a few minutes.

Add the potatoes and peas to the pressure cooker (unless you're making this dish in advance, in which case wait until just before serving). Close the lid, and bring to high pressure. Cook for a further 5 minutes, then fast release. Serve sprinkled with a little more fresh coriander.

Caribbean Mutton Curry

Having lived in the Caribbean, this is the curry I make more often than any other. I have also made this recipe with lamb and goat, but my preference is for mutton. The curry tastes very good on the day it is cooked, even better a day or so later, but absolutely sublime after it has been frozen – the savouriness intensifies somehow. This is an excellent reason to make double the amount. I have included my own curry powder mix here, but feel free to use a commercial curry powder.

1.5kg mutton or lamb shoulder or neck fillet, boned and diced into large pieces

Juice of 1 lime

3 tbsp dark rum

1 tbsp vegetable or coconut oil

2 tbsp butter

2 medium onions, sliced

2 tbsp curry powder (see recipe below or use a good ready-made one)

3 garlic cloves, crushed

2cm piece of root ginger, finely chopped

3 tomatoes, seeded and diced, or 150g tinned

1 very large thyme sprig

1 bay leaf

1 Scotch bonnet pepper

150ml coconut milk

Salt and freshly ground pepper

Place the meat in a large bowl and 'wash' it with the lime and rum (easiest done with your hands). Melt the oil and butter in the pressure cooker and add the onion. Sauté until soft and transparent. Add the curry powder, garlic and ginger and sauté for a minute more.

Add the mutton and its juices to the cooker, then pour in the tomatoes and coconut milk. Add the herbs and the Scotch bonnet pepper and season with salt and pepper. Close the lid, and bring to high pressure. Cook for 20 minutes and then allow to drop pressure naturally.

Remove the lid. Return the cooker to the heat, give everything a good stir and allow to simmer to reduce the liquid slightly. Remember to remove the Scotch bonnet before serving.

Curry Powder

5cm piece of cinnamon stick

1 tbsp coriander seed

2 tsp cumin seed

2 tsp black peppercorns

1 tsp cardamom pods

1 tsp allspice berries

½ tsp fenugreek seed

½ tsp mustard seed

2 cloves

1 large mace blade

1 tsp turmeric

1 tsp ground ginger

1 tsp cayenne pepper

Pinch of asafoetida (optional)

Put all the whole spices, including the mace, into a dry frying pan. Roast over a medium heat, shaking from time to time until the aroma of the spices becomes stronger and the mustard seed starts to pop. Remove from the heat and allow to cool. Grind the spices to a fairly fine powder with a spice grinder or pestle and mortar. Add the pre-ground spices and mix together. This will stay fresh for some time if kept away from the light in a sealed container.

Moroccan Spiced Lamb with Mint and Watermelon Salad

This recipe started off as a riff on my Pakistani mother-in-law's nod to a traditional British roast dinner – lamb, marinated in spices and yoghurt, before being slow-roasted in the oven and served as a huge slab of meat, with all the regular roast dinner trimmings. I love the yoghurt marinade, but wanted lighter, more fragrant spices, to transform it from Sunday roast to summery lunch, which is why I moved the focus from Pakistan to Morocco. Incidentally, do not throw the watermelon rind away! If you have time, you can turn it into a very refreshing jam (see page 207).

My recipe for *Ras el Hanout* (a Moroccan blend of spices) is a simple one, as a typical blend can have upwards of 30 spices in it. You can use a commercial one, but try to make sure it has rose petals in it – I find that watermelon has a hint of rose about it, so they go very well together. If you do not have time to marinate the lamb, do not worry – the pressure cooker will make sure it is still incredibly tender. In this case, don't use the yoghurt, but rub the spice mix over the lamb before browning it.

2kg lamb or mutton shoulder, boned and cut into 4 pieces

100ml plain yoghurt

2 tbsp olive oil

250ml pomegranate juice

250ml chicken stock or water

1 tbsp rose water

3 small cucumbers, topped, tailed and sliced into ribbons

¼ large watermelon, seeded and cut into fairly small chunks

3 dried rosebuds, crumbled (optional)

Finely chopped mint, to garnish

Jewelled Pilau Rice (see page 155), to serve

For the *Ras el Hanout*

Large pinch of saffron strands

1 tsp ground cardamom

1 tsp ground cumin

1 tsp ground cinnamon

1 tsp ground black pepper

1 tsp salt

¼ tsp turmeric

¼ tsp ground mace

¼ tsp ground nutmeg

6 dried rosebuds, crumbled

To make the *Ras el Hanout*, grind the saffron strands to a powder with a pestle and mortar. Combine with the rest of the spices and the rosebuds.

Put the meat in a non-metallic bowl or container. Mix the *Ras el Hanout* with the yoghurt and massage well into the meat. Leave to marinate at least overnight. (If you don't have time to marinate, omit the yoghurt and just rub in the spice mix.)

When you are ready to cook the meat, remove as much of the marinade as possible. Heat the oil in the pressure cooker and brown all the meat until seared and well caramelised. Pour over the pomegranate juice, stock and rose water. Close the lid, then bring to high pressure. Cook for 45 minutes, remove from the heat and allow to release pressure naturally.

Remove the meat from the pressure cooker. Return the cooker to the heat and simmer the cooking liquor until it has reduced to the consistency of a light syrup, then strain it. While the liquor is reducing, shred the meat with a couple of forks.

Arrange the cucumber and watermelon on a large serving platter and sprinkle over all the shredded meat. Pour over some of the reduced cooking liquor and keep the rest in a jug on the side. Decorate with finely chopped mint and crumbled rosebuds, if you like. To make this more substantial, serve with a fragrant steamed rice, such as the Jewelled Pilau Rice on page 155.

Lamb's Breast with Caper Sauce

This is one of the most challenging of cuts, and needs a bit more work than some of my other recipes. However, I include it because the meat is so incredibly cheap and full of flavour. For best results, cook one day in advance and reserve the cooking liquor, so that you can easily remove all the fat before using the liquor in the caper sauce.

4 pieces of rolled lamb breast
(each 200–250g)

150ml white wine

1 head of garlic, separated into
unpeeled cloves

1 large rosemary sprig

150ml lamb stock or water

2 tbsp olive oil (optional)

Salt and freshly ground black
and white pepper

For the stuffing

100g breadcrumbs

Grated zest of 1 lemon

2 garlic cloves, finely chopped

1 onion, finely chopped

1 rosemary sprig,
finely chopped

1 tbsp Dijon mustard

1 egg

For the caper sauce

25g butter

25g plain flour

Reserved cooking liquor,
fat removed and reserved

Splash of milk (optional)

3 tbsp capers, rinsed and
roughly chopped

First, mix all the stuffing ingredients together and season with salt and black pepper. Unroll each lamb breast and trim off any large pieces of fat. Divide the stuffing between the pieces of lamb breast and re-roll. Tie firmly with string. Put in the pressure cooker with the wine, garlic and rosemary. Add the stock or water and season everything with salt and black pepper.

Close the lid and bring to high pressure. Cook for 30 minutes then allow to drop pressure naturally. Remove the breasts from the pressure cooker. Peel the garlic cloves and mash the flesh into the cooking liquor, then strain. Cool, in order to remove most of the fat.

Make the caper sauce. Melt the butter in a pan and then add the flour. Stir together until a light golden brown and the raw smell of the flour has disappeared. Gradually whisk in the reserved cooking liquor (fat removed), adding milk towards the end if the sauce is still too thick. Season with salt and white pepper. Stir the capers into the sauce and keep warm.

Slice the lamb breasts into thick rounds (probably about three per piece). In a frying pan, heat either some of the fat skimmed from the cooking liquor or 2 tablespoons of olive oil and brown the breast pieces thoroughly until crisp and brown. Serve with the caper sauce poured over.

Stuffed Lambs' Hearts

I realise that hearts are not something many people choose to eat, but please, do give them a try. They are incredibly cheap, have a very mild taste, which makes them excellent flavour carriers, and a smooth flesh that somehow manages to be firm and tender at the same time. They are often available in supermarkets these days, ready to use, which makes them a very quick and easy option. I cooked this particular dish for my husband one Valentine's Day!

8 lambs' hearts

1 tbsp rice or potato flour (optional)

1 tbsp olive oil

25g butter

1 onion, sliced

4 garlic cloves, left unpeeled

125ml white wine

125ml lamb stock or water

1 tsp sumac

Finely chopped flat-leaf parsley, to garnish

Salt and freshly ground pepper

For the stuffing

175g lean minced lamb

1 onion, finely chopped

Grated zest of 1 lemon

2 tsp dried mint

2 tsp ground cumin

1 tsp ground coriander

1 tsp sumac

½ tsp ground cinnamon

¼ tsp cayenne pepper

If you haven't bought prepared hearts, they will need a little work before you stuff them. Cut out any obvious sinews and the ventricles (easily done with kitchen scissors), wash thoroughly to remove any blood, and trim excess fat from the opening and outside wall.

To make the stuffing, mix all the ingredients together and season with salt and pepper. I also put everything in a food processor and pulse it a few times. Stuff the lambs' hearts. Some recipes I have seen say it is necessary either to sew up the opening or secure with a skewer. I don't think this is necessary – I have never found that the stuffing falls out during the cooking process. If you like, dust the hearts in rice or potato flour – this will help them take on a good colour, but is by no means essential.

Heat the olive oil and butter in the pressure cooker over a medium heat. When the butter has melted, add the onion. Fry until lightly brown then scoop out with a slotted spoon and reserve until later. Add the hearts to the cooker. Brown them well on all sides, then make sure they are positioned with the opening facing upwards. Throw in the garlic cloves and pour over the wine and the stock or water. Season with salt and pepper.

Close the lid, then bring to high pressure. Cook for 15 minutes. Remove from the heat and allow to drop pressure naturally. When you are able to open your pressure cooker, add the onions back in. Return to the heat and boil quite vigorously to reduce the cooking liquid down into a rich, syrupy glaze. Spoon the liquid over the hearts throughout this process so that they take on some of the glossiness. When you are almost ready to serve, stir in the sumac. Serve with lots of finely chopped parsley.

Bacon and Onion Suet Roll

This pudding, a savoury take on jam roly poly, is one of those dishes that has almost been lost in the mists of time. I can't think why – it's delicious and satisfying on a cold winter's night and is also much more economical than the classic steak and kidney pudding. It is another recipe that is eminently adaptable – one of my other favourite combinations is chicken and leek, with some leftover gravy, and some butter added to the pastry.

For the pastry
150g self-raising flour
75g suet
Pinch of salt
1 tsp mustard powder

1 tsp chopped thyme leaves
Flour, for dusting

For the filling
1 onion, finely chopped

100g bacon, diced
2 generous tbsp Dijon mustard
Freshly ground black pepper

First make the pastry. Mix all the ingredients together in a bowl, then gradually add cold water until you have a firm, non-sticky dough. Roll the dough out on a floured work surface, until you have a rectangle of roughly 15cm by 30cm.

Sprinkle the surface of the dough with the onion. Mix the bacon and mustard together and sprinkle over the onion. This may seem an odd thing to do, but the flavour of the mustard will be much stronger than if you had spread it directly onto the dough. Season with black pepper. Roll up the dough, press the ends together and turn them under. Wrap in two layers of foil, crimping at both ends.

Put the steamer basket into the pressure cooker, upturned, then add 3–4cm of boiling water. Put the wrapped suet roll on top of the basket. Put on the lid without locking and allow to steam naturally for 15 minutes. Lock the lid in place, bring to high pressure then turn down the heat, enough to maintain pressure. Cook for 25 minutes. Allow to drop pressure naturally if you have time.

Unwrap and cut into thick slices. Serve with gravy (such as my Proper Gravy on page 80).

Proper Gravy

Many of the recipes in this book have their own gravy already, produced by the liquid they are cooked in. However, some of the recipes, such as the Bacon and Onion Suet Roll (see page 79) are a bit deficient in the liquor stakes. And what do you do if you fancy a good gravy with some fried sausages?

One thing some chefs advocate is to use cheaper cuts of meat solely for making gravy. I wouldn't normally do this, but sometimes I do think it's worth it, especially if you can make a fair amount and freeze it for future meals. You can also keep a bag of meat 'scraps' or trimmings in the freezer, including the pork skin used here, to cut down on the cost.

You can vary this recipe by deglazing with red wine or Marsala (for an even sweeter flavour), using trimmings from mushrooms or beef to change the flavour, or of course by changing the herbs. Smoky flavours are also good – I would consider using smoked bacon, or adding a few drops of Liquid Smoke (see page 51).

500g mixture of pork skin, meat (try belly pork) and sausagemeat, roughly chopped
50g butter

1kg onions, finely sliced
1 large thyme sprig
Pinch of bicarbonate of soda (optional)

3 fresh sage leaves, crumbled
Sherry vinegar, to taste
Salt and freshly ground pepper

Heat a frying pan and, when it is hot, add all the meat and sausagemeat. Brown thoroughly.

Put the butter in the pressure cooker and, when it is foaming, add the onions and cook with the sprig of thyme over a medium heat until caramelised. If you want to speed up this process, add a large pinch of bicarbonate of soda. Remove half the onions and add the browned meat. Deglaze the frying pan with 100ml water, allowing it to bubble up while you scrape off any bits stuck on the bottom of the cooker, and pour this into the pressure cooker too. Cover everything in the cooker with more water. Close the lid, bring to high pressure and cook for 30 minutes then allow to drop pressure naturally.

Strain the liquid into a pan and add the reserved onions. Bring to a fast simmer and reduce until taking on a light syrupy consistency. Check for seasoning, adding salt and pepper if needed, then add the crumbled sage leaves and a few drops of sherry vinegar.

Variation

Bone marrow gravy

One of the best things you can add to gravy is bone marrow. It's rich, full of flavour and is surprisingly good for you, being rich in proteins and cholesterol-lowering monounsaturated fats. The normal way to cook them (as made popular by Fergus Henderson) is to roast the bones in the oven, but if all you want to do is extract the marrow to add to gravies and sauces, or even just to eat on toast in lieu of dripping, cooking them in the pressure cooker works very well.

Ask your butcher for some thick, meaty marrow bones. Put a few centimetres of water in the base of the pressure cooker and add the trivet. Line the steamer basket with foil or put the bones into a dish that fits into the pressure cooker – this is to catch any marrow that may seep out during the cooking process. Close the lid, bring to high pressure and cook for 1 minute. Allow to release pressure naturally. You should be able to scoop out the marrow quite easily. You can now add this to the gravy recipe opposite, adding the marrow towards the end of the recipe, allowing it to simmer for 2–3 minutes.

Poultry and Game

'Don't forget that you can save any bones, trimmings and carcasses to make stock'

This chapter probably has the biggest number of interchangeable recipes. With the exception of duck, which is a much fattier bird than the rest, everything is fairly similar in terms of texture. I often swap chicken for guinea fowl, pheasant or rabbit, or partridge for pigeon, even if, in the latter case, the taste is quite dissimilar.

The method of cooking that works best with poultry and game is without a doubt pot-roasting, which helps keep the meat tender and moist. It is also the most forgiving of methods for 'tough old birds' – those old, end-of-season (or even last season!) birds that tend towards the dry and stringy. If you suspect that is the kind of bird you have, add another 5 minutes to the cooking time, make sure you are cooking it breast-side down, preferably with a good, fatty stuffing in its cavity to soak through the meat, and give it plenty of time to rest before you eat it.

If you want a crisp, brown skin on your game or poultry, you can still braise or pot-roast it, then simply finish it under a hot grill or fry in a pan. You will still be saving an inordinate amount of fuel and time than if you had conventionally roasted your bird, with the added bonus that you've got a ready-made gravy from the cooking liquid too. I frequently cook a game bird this way, then crisp up the meat and add it to salads. Try doing this with some of my Puy Lentil Salads (see page 135).

Don't forget that you can save any bones, trimmings and carcasses to make stock (see pages 18–22). Poultry stock is the most versatile and it's always handy to have some in the freezer. For this reason I very rarely buy joints of poultry. Perhaps occasionally a tray of unfilleted chicken thighs or some wings, but really there's just too much value in a whole bird to buy it any other way.

Poached Chicken

I poach a chicken in the pressure cooker when I need cooked chicken meat for another recipe, or simply want something soothing to eat. It's very quick and you can use the broth afterwards either to cook vegetables in for a kind of vegetable chicken stew (even cock–a-leekie, if you add leeks and prunes), or for any of the numerous dishes in this book that use chicken stock. Normally, I leave some fat on the chicken (usually by way of the skin on the wings) as this is collagen-rich and only adds goodness to your broth. However, I do normally skin the rest of the chicken. The discarded skin is not wasted – I will rub it with oil, sprinkle with salt then shallow fry or roast (if I already have the oven on). It's a very moreish snack, or can be broken up for savoury croutons for soups (including the broth below) or scattered over salads. Incidentally, I find that poaching in the pressure cooker is also the best way to cook chicken breasts. Off-the-bone portions take a mere 5 minutes, plus the time it takes to slow release.

1 chicken	Mixture of fresh herbs –	Salt and whole or lightly
500ml chicken stock	tarragon, curly parsley,	crushed black peppercorns
Whole garlic cloves,	bay leaves	
as many as you like		

Remove most of the skin from the chicken. Start at the neck and ease your fingers between the skin and flesh. You will find that the skin comes away very easily, the only tricky part being the wings, which I recommend leaving well alone. Put the chicken in the pressure cooker, cover with the stock and top up with water. Add the garlic cloves and herbs, a few peppercorns and ½ teaspoon of salt. Close the lid, bring to high pressure and cook for 10 minutes only. Leave to drop pressure naturally – don't open for at least 10 minutes after you have taken the cooker off the heat.

Variations

To turn into a substantial chicken broth

Follow the recipe above and prepare any vegetables you have to hand – in winter, a combination of carrots, turnips and cabbage is good; in summer, you might veer towards peas, broad beans and lettuce.

Remove the chicken from the pressure cooker and pull the meat from the bones, in large chunks. Strain the cooking liquid, mashing the garlic into the broth. Measure just half of this back into the pressure cooker and reserve the rest for other uses. Add any root vegetables at this point and cook for 2 minutes at high pressure then fast release. They should be still *al dente*. Add any other vegetables (leeks, lettuce, greens, peas, beans) and cook for 1 minute only. Again, release quickly. Return the chicken to the pressure cooker and allow everything to warm through.

Other things you can add

Some bacon or ham hock: Fry lightly and add to the pressure cooker along with the root vegetables.

Noodles: Just like minestrone, break up some spaghetti and cook under pressure with the root vegetables.

Herb oils: Take handfuls of fresh herbs (whatever you have to hand – mint, basil, coriander, parsley, tarragon), chop finely and mix with about 4 tablespoons of olive oil. Add a few finely chopped capers, a garlic clove, if you wish, and a squeeze of lemon or lime juice.

Poached Duck

I have noticed recently that poached duck, out of favour for a very long time, is having a bit of a resurgence. You can poach a duck in the pressure cooker just as easily as chicken. If it is too large to fit, cut it into pieces. I would recommend flavouring the liquor with a large bunch of mint, a few chopped garlic cloves, a clove-studded onion and a roughly chopped carrot. Cook for the same amount of time as for a chicken (see page 85), and try to remove as much of the fat from the duck as you can first.

Quick Chicken Supper for Two

I have used filleted thighs for this recipe because it's the kind of supper for which you want everything to be easy in the eating and you don't want to faff around picking meat off bones. I'm addicted to capers and add them to just about anything my husband will let me get away with, so feel free to omit them if you prefer. I love this dish served simply, with one of those floppy green lettuces that will wilt in all the tart, buttery sauce juices, no other dressing required. You will find that the skin of the chicken and potatoes stays pleasingly crisp in places.

1 tbsp olive oil

25g butter

4–6 chicken thigh fillets (depending on how hungry you are – about 500g)

3 medium waxy potatoes, cut into chunks

1 small onion, cut into quarters

4 garlic cloves, finely chopped

50ml white wine

1 tbsp Dijon mustard

1 thin slice of lemon, finely chopped

1 tbsp capers, rinsed (optional)

Large handful of basil, roughly torn

Salt and freshly ground pepper

Heat the olive oil and butter in the pressure cooker until quite hot. Add the thighs skin-side down and fry until they are well browned and have released some of their fat. Remove from the pressure cooker, add the potatoes and onion and fry until they are brown and starting to crisp around the edges. Add the garlic, stir for a few seconds, then deglaze with the white wine, allowing it to bubble up while you scrape off any bits stuck on the bottom of the cooker. Add the Dijon mustard and stir thoroughly so that it mixes well with the wine, then return the chicken to the cooker. Sprinkle over the lemon pieces and the capers, if using, then season with salt and pepper. Close the lid and bring to high pressure. Cook for 5 minutes, then remove from the heat and allow to drop pressure naturally.

Divide the chicken and vegetables between two plates. Rapidly boil the cooking juices for a couple of minutes if you think they need reducing – the mustard will act as a thickener. Add the basil to the gravy, then spoon the lot over the chicken.

Pot-roasted Chicken with Stuffing

This is the preferred way in my household of cooking and eating a whole chicken. The chicken, even the breast meat, stays tender and moist, and you have a ready-made gravy in the juices. I first made this stuffing when I needed to use up some coriander and it goes very well with the creamy, garlicky sauce. Of course you can use any type of stuffing you like. You can use this same method to cook guinea fowl.

1 free-range chicken or guinea fowl, around 1.5kg, any giblets removed
2 tbsp olive oil
Large knob of butter
200ml chicken stock or water
1 head of garlic
50ml single cream (optional)
Salt and freshly ground pepper

For the stuffing
25g butter
1 onion, finely chopped
3 garlic cloves, finely chopped
100g breadcrumbs
1 egg
Grated zest and juice of 1 lime

Handful of fresh coriander, finely chopped
Handful of curly parsley, finely chopped

First make the stuffing. Melt the butter in a frying pan and add the onion. Sauté on a low heat until the onion is translucent. Allow to cool, then add all the remaining ingredients, season with salt and pepper and mix thoroughly. Stuff the chicken with the mixture.

Heat up the olive oil and butter in the pressure cooker. Add the stuffed chicken and carefully brown it on all sides, paying particular attention to the breasts. Place the chicken right-way up, then add the stock or water. Break up the head of garlic and put the unpeeled cloves around the chicken. Season with salt and pepper. Lock the lid and bring up to full pressure. Turn down the heat and maintain high pressure for 20 minutes. Let the pressure lower naturally at room temperature.

Remove the chicken to a serving plate and cover. Mash the garlic cloves into the remaining cooking liquor. Add any liquid that drains from the chicken, and the cream, if using. Strain into a jug and serve with the chicken.

Chicken with Red Peppers, Capers and Black Olives

To speed this dish up even more, you can use filleted chicken thighs, then cook at high pressure for just 4 minutes. If you want to add more meat, a couple of cooking chorizos would work very well. Slice them into chunks on the diagonal and fry at the beginning, before the chicken, reducing the oil to 1 teaspoon (the chorizo will produce a lot of its own fat). I have also made this very successfully with rabbit. Using lime to 'wash' chicken is a tip I learned in the Caribbean – similarly to lemon, it adds depth and helps to bring out the savoury flavours. You can substitute with lemon if you like.

---

1 chicken (about 1.5kg), jointed into 8 pieces, or a mixture of chicken pieces, skinned

Juice of 1 lime

3 tbsp olive oil

1 red onion, cut lengthways into wedges

4 garlic cloves, chopped

50ml white wine

2 large rosemary sprigs

1 tsp dried sage

200g tinned chopped tomatoes or 4 fresh tomatoes

2 red peppers, skinned (see method on page 182) and cut into strips

50g pitted black olives, halved

2 tbsp capers, rinsed

Salt and freshly ground pepper

Finely chopped parsley, to garnish

Sautéed potatoes, to serve

Rub the chicken all over with the lime juice. Heat the olive oil in the pressure cooker. Turn up the heat to high, add the chicken pieces and brown them – you may need to do this in two batches. Remove the chicken and add the onion and garlic to the cooker. Sauté for a minute. Pour in the wine and stir vigorously to deglaze, scraping up any bits stuck on the bottom of the cooker. Add the rosemary and sage, then return the chicken pieces to the pan, season with salt and black pepper and add the tomatoes.

Close the lid and bring to high pressure. Cook for 10 minutes then allow to lose pressure naturally. Remove the chicken from the pressure cooker onto a warmed serving plate. Return the cooker to a high heat, add the red peppers, olives and capers and boil for a couple of minutes to let the flavours marry and the juices reduce slightly. Serve the chicken with the sauce spooned over it, scattered with the chopped parsley. This is delicious with sautéed potatoes.

Chicken and Cashew Nut Curry
(Parsi Kaju na Murgh)

This recipe was given to me by Indian-born Geordie food writer Maunika Gowardhan, a very knowledgeable cook who staved off homesickness when she first moved to the UK by cooking some of her mother's and grandmother's dishes. Don't be worried by the number of chillies used here – Kashmiri chillies are particularly mild and used for the deep-red colour they impart. If you can't get hold of them, Maunika suggests substituting a heaped teaspoon of mild paprika and ⅓ teaspoon of cayenne pepper.

10–12 whole dried Kashmiri red chillies, seeded

50g cashew nuts

7 garlic cloves

3cm piece of root ginger

2 tbsp vegetable oil

1 tsp cumin seed

4 cloves

1 bay leaf

1 large onion, finely sliced

1kg chicken pieces, skinned but left on the bone

2 tbsp tomato purée

Pinch of sugar

Salt and freshly ground pepper

Chopped fresh coriander, to garnish

Chapatis and green salad, to serve

Soak the chillies and cashew nuts in separate bowls of warm water for 15–20 minutes. Drain the chillies and put in a food processor with the garlic, ginger and a couple of tablespoons of the soaking water. Blitz until you have a thick paste. Remove and set aside. Drain the cashew nuts and also process them with a little of their soaking water in the cleaned food processor until they form a paste.

Heat the vegetable oil in the pressure cooker, add the cumin seed, cloves and bay leaf and fry for a few moments. Add the onion slices and cook on a medium heat, stirring frequently until they have softened and started to turn golden brown. Now add the chilli paste and cook for another 2–3 minutes, continuing to stir. Put the chicken pieces in the cooker and, turning frequently, cook until they have started to brown and are thoroughly coated in the spice mix. Add 200ml water and season with salt and pepper.

Close the lid and when high pressure is reached, cook for 5 minutes. Allow the pressure to drop naturally, then remove the lid and add the tomato purée, sugar and cashew nut paste. Simmer for a couple of minutes until the sauce has thickened. Serve with a generous garnish of chopped coriander. Great with chapatis and a green salad.

Pheasant Fesenjan

This is a special-occasion Persian dish which is definitely better the day after cooking. I use pheasant in this recipe, as it is commonly used in Iran, but you can easily substitute it with something else – chicken, duck and lamb/mutton all work very well. An Iranian friend tells me that her mother regularly used meatballs, favouring the Swedish variety!

Pomegranate molasses is now readily available in the UK. You don't need much for this recipe, but don't let that deter you from trying it – the molasses can be used for all kinds of other things, including marinades and salad dressings. Fesenjan is traditionally served with a plain steamed rice, but I prefer to serve it with a herby pilau with broad beans (see introduction to Jewelled Pilau Rice on page 155).

50g butter

2 pheasants (each around 600–800g), both jointed into 4 pieces

1 onion, finely chopped

150g walnuts, finely ground

3 tbsp pomegranate molasses

300ml stock (preferably chicken)

½ tsp ground cinnamon

1 bay leaf

Pinch of sugar

Salt and freshly ground pepper

Chopped flat-leaf parsley, to garnish

Pilau rice, to serve (see above)

Heat the butter in the base of the pressure cooker. Once it has melted and started to foam, add the pheasant pieces and brown on all sides. When they are a good colour, remove from the pressure cooker. Add the onion and walnuts and fry until the onions have started to take on a light colour. Add the pomegranate molasses, stock, cinnamon, bay leaf, sugar and seasoning.

If you want your sauce fairly smooth, this is a good time to give it a quick whiz with a hand blender if you have one. Then return the pheasant pieces to the pan, close the lid and bring to high pressure. Cook for 15 minutes then release pressure naturally.

Leave on a low heat to simmer, until the sauce has reduced and has turned into a thick gravy. When you are ready to serve, sprinkle over the chopped parsley. Serve with pilau rice.

Guinea Fowl or Rabbit with Saffron, Oregano and Lemon

This is adapted from one of my mother's favourite recipes. She uses rabbit or chicken normally, so it makes sense that it works with guinea fowl too. As my parents live in Greece, it is easy for her to get dried, unopened oregano buds, and while they are available here, dried oregano or marjoram leaf is a very good substitution. Whipping cream is used as it is less likely to curdle than double cream (although it doesn't matter too much if it does).

Large pinch of saffron

2 tbsp olive oil

1 rabbit or large guinea fowl (about 1kg), jointed and skinned

150ml whipping cream

2 generous tsp dried oregano flower buds or 1 tsp dried oregano leaf

2 tbsp Dijon mustard

50ml white wine

Juice of 1 lemon

100ml water or stock (poultry or game is good)

Pinch of cayenne pepper

4–6 cooked artichoke hearts (from a jar is fine)

Salt and freshly ground pepper

Sautéed potatoes, to serve

Mix the saffron in a little warm water and leave to infuse.

Put the olive oil in the pressure cooker. When hot, add the guinea fowl or rabbit pieces and brown on all sides. Arrange the joints so that the meatiest sections rest on the base of the pressure cooker. Take 50ml of the cream and mix it with the saffron liquid and all the other ingredients, except the artichoke hearts. Pour this over the browned meat.

Close the lid and bring to high pressure. Cook for 10 minutes and allow to drop pressure naturally. Add the artichoke hearts and the rest of the cream and simmer over a very low heat for a few minutes, then serve with sautéed potatoes.

Pigeon with Bacon and Peas

This has always been my favourite way to eat pigeon – its gaminess makes the dish taste a little bit like a superior dish of liver and bacon. I know the peas have a very long cooking time here, but although they lose their fresh greenness, they instead become incredibly sweet and soft. Instead of the redcurrant or herb jelly, you could use my Sloe and Apple Jelly (see page 213).

1 tbsp olive oil

25g butter

12 button onions, blanched for 2 minutes in boiling water and then peeled

100g streaky bacon lardons

2 garlic cloves, finely chopped

4 large pigeons (250–300g each)

150ml red wine

50ml poultry or game stock

2 bay leaves

1 tsp juniper berries, roughly crushed

300g fresh or frozen peas

1 tsp redcurrant or herb jelly (optional)

Salt and freshly ground pepper

Mashed potatoes or Crushed Carrots and Swede (see page 168), to serve

Heat the olive oil and butter in the pressure cooker. When the butter is foaming, add the blanched button onions and fry until browned to the point of caramelising. Remove from the pressure cooker.

Fry the bacon lardons until crisp, then add the garlic and pigeons. Brown the pigeons quickly on all sides and leave upside down. Pour over the red wine and stock, and tuck in the bay leaves. Season with salt and pepper. Close the lid, bring to high pressure and cook for 10–15 minutes, depending on the age of the bird (ask your butcher, as older ones will take longer). Allow to drop pressure naturally.

Add the peas and the browned button onions to the cooker, then close the lid once more and cook for 2 minutes, again allowing the pressure to drop naturally. Keep simmering to reduce the sauce down a little. Taste for seasoning and add salt and pepper if needed. You might also want to add a little redcurrant, herb or Sloe and Apple jelly if you think it could do with a bit more sweetness. Good with mashed potatoes, or with the Crushed Carrots and Swede on page 168.

Partridge with Chorizo Stuffing

We tend to think of game birds being very traditionally British, but we are wrong to do so – they're popular throughout the world, and partridges particularly so in Spain. This recipe gives a nod to that, with its chorizo stuffing, and gutsy, red wine sauce. You could also use white beans instead of the chickpeas.

2 large or 4 small partridges (800g–1kg in total)

2 tbsp olive oil, plus more for the cabbage

1 onion, finely chopped

2 garlic cloves

½ tsp sweet paprika

½ tsp hot paprika

1 thyme sprig

100ml red wine

100ml chicken or game stock, or water

1 very ripe tomato, chopped

200g cooked chickpeas (see method on page 132)

½ savoy cabbage (optional), shredded

Butter, for the cabbage

Salt and freshly ground pepper

For the stuffing

75g *picante* cooking chorizo, very finely chopped

1 leek, finely chopped

2 garlic cloves, chopped

1 tsp finely chopped flat-leaf parsley

100g breadcrumbs

Make the stuffing: put the chorizo in a warmed frying pan and cook over a medium heat until much of the oil has been released and the pieces are well browned. Drain off most of the oil and add the leek and garlic. Sauté for a minute, then remove from the heat. Stir in the parsley and breadcrumbs and season with salt and pepper. When the stuffing is cool enough to handle, use it to stuff the cavities of the birds.

Heat the olive oil in the pressure cooker and brown the birds on all sides. Add the onion and garlic and leave to soften for a couple of minutes, then sprinkle over both types of paprika and tuck in the thyme sprig. Pour over the red wine and stock or water, add the tomato and season with salt and pepper. Turn the partridges upside down and make sure they are well embedded in the cooking liquids.

Close the lid and bring to high pressure. Cook for 15 minutes then allow to drop pressure naturally. Add the chickpeas to the pressure cooker and allow to warm through.

I also like to include the shredded savoy cabbage, which I start off in a frying pan, sautéing it in butter and olive oil until it starts to go brown at the edges. Add to the pressure cooker to finish cooking through.

Spiced Duck à l'Orange

A recipe adapted from Rick Stein's *Far Eastern Odyssey*, which captured my imagination and is probably the best duck recipe I've ever tasted. It even converted my husband, who does not normally like orange in savoury dishes. I've toned down the star anise a little, as it's a flavour I think is best when muted. Serve simply with some wilted Chinese greens (see page 172) and steamed basmati or jasmine rice.

1 duck, jointed into 8 (or 2 breasts and 2 legs, all cut in half)

1 head of garlic, separated into cloves and finely chopped

50g root ginger, chopped

500ml fresh orange juice

2 tbsp fish sauce

2 tsp sugar

1 star anise

2 bird's-eye red chillies

2 lemongrass stalks, finely chopped

8 spring onions, cut into white and green parts

Freshly ground pepper

Heat the pressure cooker without adding any oil or fat. When it is hot, add the duck pieces, skin-side down and fry until a lot of their own fat has been released and the skin is crisp and a deep golden brown. You may have to do this in batches.

Remove all but a couple of tablespoons of the fat (put in the fridge for another use). Add the garlic and ginger and fry until starting to take on some colour. Add all the remaining ingredients except the spring onions and season with lots of black pepper. Return the duck to the pan, close the lid and bring to high pressure. Cook for 30 minutes, then allow to drop pressure naturally.

Cut the white parts of the spring onions in half lengthways. Add to the pressure cooker and simmer until soft. Remove the duck pieces from the pressure cooker and keep warm. Skim off any excess fat (there will probably be plenty) and leave the cooking liquor to reduce until thicker and syrupy.

Shred the green parts of the spring onions lengthways and serve the duck with them sprinkled over the top.

Rabbit in a Thai Red Curry

Thai curries are wonderful with game, especially as coconut milk helps to add richness. I also like using red curry paste with duck, and I have it on good authority that yellow curry paste is good with rabbit. My recipe for red curry paste is based on the one in David Thompson's authoritative *Thai Food*. If you don't want the hassle of making your own, then a good ready-made one would do.

400ml tin of coconut milk

100ml chicken stock or water

1 rabbit, jointed

1 tbsp vegetable oil

1 tsp palm sugar
  (use soft light brown
  sugar if you can't get this)

2 tbsp fish sauce

4 kaffir lime leaves, shredded

2–3 green chillies, seeded and
  thinly sliced into rounds

Handful of basil or coriander

Steamed jasmine rice, to serve

For the red curry paste

5 dried Kashmiri
  chillies, soaked

3 lemongrass stalks, tough
  outer layer removed,
  insides finely chopped

1 shallot, finely chopped

4 garlic cloves, finely chopped

1 tsp white peppercorns

½ tsp shrimp paste

1 tsp ground coriander

1 tsp ground cumin

½ tsp turmeric

Large pinch of ground cloves

2 kaffir lime leaves, or pared
  zest of 1 kaffir lime

Make the red curry paste by grinding all the ingredients together in a small food processor. Add a little water to help this along.

Put the coconut milk and stock in the pressure cooker along with the rabbit. Close the lid and bring to high pressure. Cook for around 15 minutes, then slow release.

Heat the vegetable oil in a frying pan and fry 3 tablespoons of the paste in it. Add this to the rabbit, deglaze the frying pan with a little water, allowing it to bubble up while you scrape off any bits stuck on the bottom of the cooker, then add this too. Add the palm sugar and fish sauce and simmer until everything is amalgamated. Stir in the lime leaves, chillies and herbs and then serve with steamed jasmine rice.

Pigeon Masala

I was surprised to hear from my mother-in-law that all the game birds we consider resolutely European have always been very popular in Pakistan. She usually uses pigeon or partridge for this recipe. You can use any kind of garam masala; I have included a recipe, but these days even my mother-in-law uses a ready-made one. She tells me that the reason the masala is mixed with water, instead of being fried with the onion and whole spices, is to give the dish a lighter colour.

Vegetable oil or ghee	1 tbsp single cream or 2 tbsp milk	4 pigeons
2 medium onions, finely chopped	4 cardamom pods	60ml plain yoghurt
2 tbsp garam masala (see recipe below or use ready-made)	3 cloves	Green chillies, sliced into rounds, and/or coriander leaves, to garnish
	4cm piece of cinnamon stick	

Coat the base of the pressure cooker with a thin layer of vegetable oil or ghee. Add the chopped onions and fry until they're golden brown. Meanwhile, mix the garam masala in around 125ml water and the cream or milk and stir thoroughly. Set aside for a moment.

Add the spices to the pressure cooker and let them splutter in the oil, then, stirring as you do so, add the masala cream mixture to the cooker. Pierce the pigeons' skin in several places with a sharp knife tip, then add to the pressure cooker. Coat with the spicy liquid. Make sure the pigeons are breast-side down, then close the lid. Bring to high pressure and cook for 15 minutes, then allow to drop pressure naturally.

Add the yoghurt to the sauce and simmer for a few minutes to allow all the flavours to meld together. Sprinkle with green chillies and/or coriander leaves to serve.

Garam Masala

5cm piece of cinnamon stick	1 tsp green cardamom pods	1 mace blade
1 dried bay leaf	2 black cardamom pods	½ tsp nigella seed
4 cloves	1 tsp cumin seed	½ tsp cayenne pepper
1 tsp black peppercorns	1 tsp coriander seed	½ tsp turmeric

Don't bother toasting the ingredients, just grind them all together and keep in an airtight container. Use as needed.

Fish and Seafood

'The pressure cooker can be indispensable with certain types of fish'

The pressure cooker must be used very discriminately when it comes to fish and seafood. Certain fish are very delicate and will disintegrate if cooked in liquid under high pressure. Most crustaceans and molluscs need so little cooking that there is no point in using the pressure cooker – they will overcook in seconds, resulting in either a rubbery or pappy texture that nobody will enjoy.

However, the pressure cooker can be indispensable with certain types of fish. Tough stuff like octopus, squid and cuttlefish can be stewed in a fraction of the time normally needed to make them tender. I tenderise conch (and their substitute, whelks) for use in Caribbean curries and fritters. Firm-fleshed fish (i.e., not those that flake readily, so don't use cod or haddock, for instance) are wonderful in curries, tagines and traditional soups. Large crustaceans such as lobster and crab can be cooked in 2–3 minutes by steaming on a medium pressure, which saves enormously on time, water and fuel.

You can also use the pressure cooker to cook fish 'en papillote', something normally done in the oven. The cooking times for this are such that you can easily cook rice or potatoes in the pressure cooker along with the fish, thereby saving even more time, fuel and washing-up. For example, if I am cooking fish in a parcel with Chinese aromatics, I usually have rice simmering away underneath.

You will notice that I haven't specified what kind of fish to use in some of these recipes. That's because I am very aware of the issues surrounding the sustainability of fish, and the list of what we should and should not be eating is constantly changing. For the purposes of pressure cooking, I tend to avoid any fish that breaks up too easily, such as cod and haddock; I have been experimenting with gurnard, tilapia, pouting and whiting. Just remember that for all the steamed or 'en papillote' recipes, it is the thickness of the fish and whether it is on or off the bone that is more important than the type. Anything around 2cm thick will take around 5 minutes – add another 2 minutes if it is a whole fish on the bone. You can also cook fish from frozen – just add another minute to the cooking time.

Remember also that the pressure cooker can be used to make fish dishes in which the fish is added at the last minute. I use it to make bouillon (fish stock, enriched with white wine); I also use the Sardine Curry recipe (see page 111) as a base but instead add white fish, or make a very simple Thai curry, cooking the vegetables (usually potatoes and pea aubergines) at pressure before adding the fish.

Fish 'en Papillote'

This is fish cooked in a parcel. You can use greaseproof paper, foil or exotic things like banana leaves to wrap the fish; open at the table and an enticing steam cloud of delicately cooked fish and aromatics will hit you. If I use whole fish, I cut slashes into their sides and stuff the aromatics in and around them. You can use steaks or fillets as well. Just remember that the general rule of thumb is to cook your fish for around 6 minutes for a piece of fish 2.5–3cm thick. Increase this by a couple of minutes if it's thicker or if you are cooking fish on the bone. You can also cook fish from frozen as long as you add another minute to the cooking time.

Normally when I cook fish in this way, I will cook either rice or potatoes in the main body of the pressure cooker and put the fish in the steamer basket. I will also sometimes slice the potatoes very thinly and put them in the steamer basket under the fish parcels. This works if you are cooking thicker pieces of fish or fish on the bone. If the fish only needs 6 minutes, I first steam the potatoes at high pressure for 3–4 minutes before adding the fish parcels.

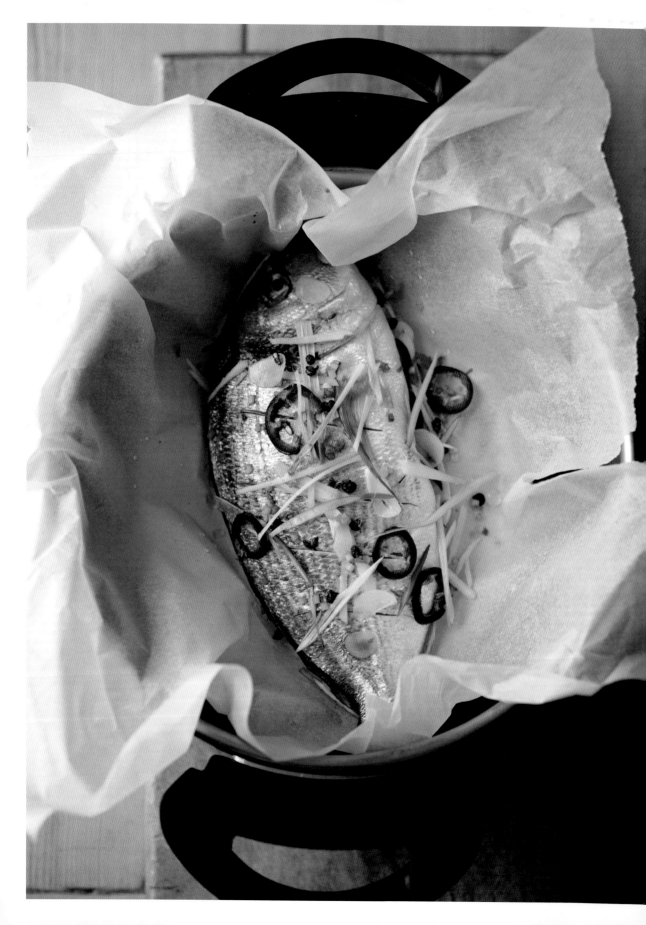

Chinese-style Fish 'en Papillote'

The rice and fish unadorned are delicate and aromatic – if you want something heartier, add the sauce as well.

200g long-grain rice, well rinsed (optional)

¼ tsp salt

4 small sea bream or equivalent (see page 104), scaled and gutted

Vegetable oil, for greasing

2 garlic cloves, very thinly sliced

3cm piece of root ginger, very thinly sliced

1 spring onion, cut into tiny batons

1 red chilli, seeded and finely sliced

1 tsp Szechuan peppercorns (or pink peppercorns if you can't get them)

1 tbsp finely chopped coriander stems

2 tbsp rice wine or rice wine vinegar

For the sauce (optional)

2 tbsp vegetable oil

1cm piece of root ginger, finely shredded into batons

1 spring onion, finely shredded into batons

2 tbsp chopped coriander leaves

Pinch of sugar

2 tbsp soy sauce

1 tsp sesame oil

If you are cooking rice at the same time as the fish, put it in the base of the pressure cooker and cover with 300ml water. Sprinkle with the salt.

Put the trivet in the pressure cooker. Cut two pieces of greaseproof paper, each big enough to hold half the fish, and oil lightly. If you are using whole fish, you may want to cut off the heads and tails, but if they fit, I prefer to leave them whole (I like the cheek meat). Cut slashes in the skin on each side. Sprinkle half the garlic, ginger, spring onion, chilli, peppercorns and coriander stems over the paper, place the fish on top and sprinkle with the remaining garlic, etc., tucking some inside the fish. Pour over the rice wine. Seal the parcels and place in the pressure cooker on the trivet. They will stack up quite well.

Close the lid and bring to high pressure. Cook for as long as necessary (see introduction on page 105) and allow to drop pressure naturally.

While you are waiting for the pressure to drop, make the sauce, if you are using it. Heat the vegetable oil in a shallow pan until smoking hot. Throw in the ginger and spring onion and allow to sizzle. Just before you are ready to serve, add everything else, swish round quickly to combine and pour over the rice and fish.

Fish 'en Papillote' with Leeks and Saffron Butter Sauce

This is one dish to which I like to add potatoes. Either add whole new potatoes to the main body of water (best if your fish is only going to take 5–6 minutes to cook) or slice them fairly thinly and cook them in the steamer basket, under the fish.

2 tbsp pine nuts
50g butter
1 tbsp olive oil

2 leeks, white parts only, finely sliced into rounds
4 pieces of fish, whole, fillets or steaks

4 tbsp sherry
Large pinch of saffron
Salt and freshly ground pepper

Put the pine nuts in a frying pan and dry roast until they take on some colour, then remove and set aside. Heat the butter and olive oil in the same pan and, when the butter is foaming, add the leeks. Sauté for 3–4 minutes just to get them started. Season well with salt and pepper, then arrange between as many parcels as you decide you need (see instructions on page 107).

Place the fish on top of the leeks and season again. Deglaze the pan with the sherry, allowing it to bubble up while you scrape off any bits stuck on the bottom of the pan, then add the saffron. Swirl around for a minute, letting it bubble up, then pour this over the fish. Seal the parcels and put in the steamer basket. Cook at high pressure for as long as necessary (see page 105 for timings) and allow to drop pressure naturally. Serve the fish sprinkled with the toasted pine nuts.

Sardines

Everyone in my family has a fondness for tinned sardines, especially in tomato sauce. Of course, we love fresh sardines too, especially grilled or barbecued, but the children prefer the tinned variety because the bones are soft. They are made commercially through a type of pressure steaming and I was intrigued to realise that the same results can be achieved at home.

I'm sure some of you are thinking – why bother? Aren't canned sardines usually as cheap as chips and fresh ones more expensive? I did a price compare and found that per 100g, fresh sardines often work out at either a similar price or cheaper. Cooking them yourself also means that you have complete control over the sauce in which you eat them. Of course, it's not quite as convenient as opening a can, but they do store well in the freezer and you can even pack them into sterilised jars and cook under pressure for 20 minutes in order to preserve them.

I give a couple of options here. One is a tomato sauce to which you can easily add chilli. Another is a curry, which is absolutely wonderful wrapped up in a roti because you don't have to worry about bones and so can wolf the lot down. You could also cook the sardines in olive oil or a fish bouillon with cider vinegar or verjuice added to it for a good tang.

Sardines in Tomato Sauce

The sardines will take longer than usual to cook in this sauce because of the tomato, which inhibits the bone softening.

1kg small sardines or other oily fish, gutted and heads removed
1 onion, finely chopped
5 garlic cloves, finely sliced

400g tin of chopped tomatoes (or 8 fresh)
100ml red wine or water
2 bay leaves

1 tsp sweet paprika
Chipotle powder or hot paprika to spice it up (optional)
Salt and freshly ground pepper

Put the sardines in a bowl and cover with 50g salt and 500ml water. Leave to soak for 15 minutes – this is to help draw the blood out of them. Rinse thoroughly.

Add all the other ingredients to the pressure cooker, along with ½ teaspoon of salt and lots of black pepper. Rinse the empty tomato tin out with a splash of water and pour this in too. Immerse the sardines in the sauce ingredients. Close the lid, bring to high pressure and cook for 20 minutes for small sardines, or up to 45 minutes for larger ones. Release pressure naturally.

Sardine Curry

You can also use this curry sauce for other types of fish. Follow the instructions, but instead of adding the sardines, add thick white fish fillets or steaks and cook at high pressure for 1 minute only. Allow to drop pressure naturally. The fish will continue to cook while the pressure drops.

1kg small sardines or other oily fish, gutted and heads removed

4 cloves

3cm piece of cinnamon stick

1 tsp coriander seed

1 tsp cumin seed

½ tsp fenugreek seed

1 tsp black peppercorns

6 dried red Kashmiri chillies, soaked (or 1 tsp cayenne pepper)

5 garlic cloves, roughly chopped

2 small onions, 1 roughly chopped, the other sliced into thin crescents

1 tsp turmeric

75g creamed coconut (the oil from this can be used as the coconut oil, below)

2 tbsp coconut or vegetable oil

1 tbsp tomato purée

2 tbsp tamarind concentrate

150g cooked chickpeas (optional)

Coriander leaves, roughly torn, to garnish

1 lemon, cut into wedges, to serve

Chapatis or other roti breads, to serve

Put the sardines in a bowl and cover with 50g salt and 500ml water. Leave to soak for 15 minutes – this is to help draw the blood out of them. Rinse thoroughly.

In a frying pan, toast the whole spices. When they start to release their aromas, remove, allow to cool a little and then grind in a spice grinder. Put the soaked chillies, garlic and roughly chopped onion in a food processor with half the creamed coconut and blend to a paste. Add the ground spices and turmeric and blend again.

Heat the oil in the base of the pressure cooker. Add the paste and fry for a couple of minutes, then add the remaining creamed coconut, the tomato purée and tamarind concentrate. Pour in 200ml water and combine. Add the sardines and immerse. Close the lid, bring to high pressure and cook for 20 minutes for small sardines, or up to 45 minutes for larger ones. Release pressure naturally then add the chickpeas if you are using them.

Serve the curry wrapped in warm chapatis, with coriander leaves, the raw onion crescents and lemon wedges for squeezing.

Fennel and Fish Tagine

For this dish to work, you need a firm-textured fish that will not flake – monkfish is ideal, but often prohibitively expensive; I have had equal success with tilapia.

750g fish, filleted and cut into large chunks

2–3 tbsp olive oil

Knob of butter

1 leek, finely diced

1 carrot, finely diced

1 celery stick, finely diced

2 large fennel bulbs

¼–½ preserved lemon (depending on how much sourness you like), finely chopped

2 large fresh tomatoes, peeled, seeded and finely chopped

500ml fish stock

500g small new or salad potatoes, cut in half lengthways

Juice of ½ lemon

Bunch of mint, roughly shredded

1 tsp ouzo or Pernod (optional)

Salt and freshly ground pepper

For the chermoula

3 garlic cloves, roughly chopped

1 red chilli, seeded and roughly chopped

1 tsp sea salt

25g chopped coriander, stalks and leaves

Pinch of saffron

2 tsp ground cumin

4 tbsp olive oil

Juice of 1 lemon

Pound the chermoula ingredients together, either with a heavy pestle and mortar, or in a food processor. Reserve 2 teaspoons of the chermoula and pour the rest over the fish, coating thoroughly. Leave to marinate for at least a couple of hours.

Put 2 tablespoons of olive oil and most of the butter in the base of the pressure cooker and heat until the butter is foaming. Add the leek, carrot and celery and cook over a medium heat until the vegetables just start to caramelise. Meanwhile, prepare the fennel by trimming away any fronds and a small amount of the base. Cut into quarters, making sure that the pieces are still attached together at the bottom.

Remove the vegetables from the pressure cooker, add slightly more oil and butter if necessary, then sauté the fennel quarters until also starting to caramelise. Return the other vegetables to the pressure cooker, along with the preserved lemon, tomatoes, stock, potatoes and the reserved chermoula. Season with salt and pepper. Close the lid and bring to high pressure, then cook for 3 minutes. Remove from the heat and fast release. Check the fennel and potatoes – they should be almost cooked through.

You can cook the fish in one of two ways. Place it on top of the contents of the pressure cooker, along with the rest of its marinade, then either close the lid, bring up to pressure and cook for 30 seconds exactly before fast releasing, or bring the contents of the pressure cooker to a simmer without the lid and let the fish cook conventionally for a few minutes.

When you are ready to serve, add the lemon juice, shredded mint and the teaspoon of ouzo or Pernod, if you like, to bring out the flavour of the fennel. Leave to stand for a couple of minutes and then ladle into bowls.

Basque Squid Stew

I have been making this stew regularly ever since it first appeared in Rick Stein's *Fruits of the Sea*. There are two ways to cook squid – either very fast on a high heat, or slow, so that it becomes tender and buttery. The pressure cooker speeds up this latter process enormously.

You can use this recipe as a base for a hearty meal and add more fish and seafood to it right at the end. You can also add other flavours – fennel is good, as is chilli and/or paprika. You could reduce the sauce down further and stir through some pasta, or you could do what I normally do – wolf the lot down with some buttered, toasted sourdough.

1 tbsp olive oil
25g butter
750g cleaned squid, cut into rings
1 onion, finely chopped

3 garlic cloves, finely chopped
400g tin of chopped tomatoes
150ml red wine
1 tsp fresh thyme leaves

½ tsp salt
Freshly ground pepper
Chopped flat-leaf parsley, to garnish

Heat the oil and butter in the pressure cooker. When the butter is foaming, add the squid and cook over a high heat until it is golden brown. Add the onion and garlic and cook for another 2 minutes.

Add all the remaining ingredients to the cooker, season with the salt and black pepper, close the lid, bring to high pressure and cook for 20 minutes. Allow to release pressure naturally. Simmer for a couple of minutes then allow to rest for another 5 minutes before eating. Sprinkle with chopped parsley to serve.

Whelks Braised with Bacon and White Beans

Whelks are a true love/hate thing, but I do think that many people who profess to hate them actually just hate the idea of them. I wish more people would try them – they're cheap, plentiful, surprisingly versatile and, more to the point, they taste good! I use them as a substitute for their larger, Caribbean cousin, the conch, which is hard to get in the UK, for Caribbean recipes such as conch fritters and curry. I also like them braised, Chinese-style, or boiled up and eaten with malt vinegar and ground white pepper, or dipped in aïoli. I often buy whelks ready-cooked and removed from their shell, but it is better to buy them in their shells.

250g whelks

75g bacon lardons

200g cannellini beans, unsoaked

2 bay leaves

1 tbsp vegetable oil

4 garlic cloves, chopped

2 red chillies, seeded and finely chopped

1 tbsp tomato purée

1 tsp sweet paprika

1 tbsp sherry

Salt and freshly ground pepper

Chopped flat-leaf parsley, to garnish

To cook the whelks, put in the pressure cooker, cover with water (make sure you do not go above the ⅔ mark), add a teaspoon of salt (and other aromatics if you like) and cook at high pressure for 5 minutes. Allow to drop pressure naturally. They will be very easy to remove from the shells, just make sure that you remove the 'operculum' – impossible to miss, it's the thin, hard bit attached to the foot of the whelk. Give the whelks a rinse and they're ready to use. You can leave them whole or chop them roughly for this dish.

Fry the bacon lardons in the pressure cooker. Remove when they are nicely browned. Put the cannellini beans and bay leaves in the cooker with 750ml water. Add ½ teaspoon of salt and the vegetable oil. Close the lid and bring to high pressure. Cook for 15 minutes, then fast release.

Add the whelks, bacon, garlic, chillies, tomato purée and paprika to the pressure cooker. Close the lid again and cook for another 15 minutes then allow to drop pressure naturally. Add the sherry, simmer for a couple more minutes, then serve sprinkled with chopped parsley.

Greek Octopus Salad

This is a staple of the Greek meze or 'small plate' table. Octopus is readily available in the UK either fresh or frozen. I buy it frozen as this helps to tenderise the rather tough meat. Another benefit of buying frozen octopus is that it will usually have already been cleaned. If buying fresh, I would strongly recommend you freeze it for a couple of weeks before cooking it. This salad is also good with a few steamed new potatoes added to it.

---

1 large octopus, preferably frozen

1 onion, cut into quarters

A few garlic cloves, left unpeeled but pierced with the tip of a knife

75ml red wine

1 bay leaf

1 tsp fennel seed

1 tsp black peppercorns

Pinch of salt

For the vinaigrette

6 tbsp extra virgin olive oil

4 tbsp red wine vinegar

1 tsp ouzo, or another aniseed-based spirit

2 shallots, thinly sliced into crescents

1 fennel, halved and thinly sliced, fronds reserved

Salt and freshly ground pepper

Put your octopus into the pressure cooker with all the other ingredients (except those for the vinaigrette), and 100ml water. If you are cooking the octopus from frozen, cook at high pressure for 15 minutes; if you are cooking a defrosted octopus, cook for 12 minutes. Allow the pressure to drop naturally and leave the octopus to cool to room temperature. When it has done so, rinse under cold water, rubbing off any flaky bits of dark skin. Cut into chunks.

While the octopus is cooling, make the vinaigrette. Whisk together the oil, vinegar and ouzo with an additional 2 tablespoons of water. Season with salt and pepper and taste. Adjust the quantities according to your preference, but the vinegar should be quite strong. Add the shallots and fennel, including any feathery fronds of the latter. Add the octopus and lightly fold until coated in the vinaigrette.

Leave to marinate in the fridge for at least a couple of hours, then serve at room temperature.

Beans and Pulses

'Cook beans and pulses very quickly, with no need to pre-soak'

Whenever I've written about using pressure cookers in the past, it is always the ability to cook beans and pulses very quickly, with no need to pre-soak, that gets people most excited. Not only do you save a huge amount of time, but you can save a small fortune on fuel and buying dried beans and pulses instead of the ready-cooked, salted ones available in tins and cartons.

One of the biggest questions regarding beans is whether or not to soak them. I tend not to, as while soaking helps to remove those difficult carbohydrates that cause flatulence, it also results in the loss of vitamins, minerals and flavour. However, in most recipes I do include cooking instructions for both soaked and unsoaked beans as I know a fair few people will disagree with me, or will simply want to save even more time during the cooking process. If you choose to, soak overnight, or follow the packet instructions. Soaking is unnecessary in some cases; most lentils take a short time anyway, it doesn't make much sense to soak them. This applies to some beans too – black eyed beans take a mere 6–8 minutes when cooked from unsoaked.

Cooked beans and lentils are some of the most useful things to have lying around if you want quick and economical meals. I work on the principle that if I'm cooking them for one meal, I may as well save fuel and cook double in the same amount of time. Therefore the minimum I tend to cook at a time is 500g, half for the recipe and the rest for something else. I use them to bulk out soups, curries and even sauces (adding brown lentils to a ragù makes your meat go much further, adds a creaminess in texture and also sneaks more goodness into the meal, perfect when you are feeding children), make salads with beans and lentils, turn chickpeas or broad beans into Hummus (see page 47) or falafel – the possibilities are endless.

If a recipe calls for draining the beans, consider keeping the cooking liquor. It will take on the flavours of any aromatics you have used but will also contain some of the starch released from the beans. This normally has a lovely nutty, creamy flavour and will help to thicken any soup in which you use it.

There are two important rules to follow when cooking beans and pulses:

1. Never fill the pressure cooker beyond the halfway mark, including with water, when cooking beans from scratch.

2. Always remember to add the oil as stated in the recipe.

This is because pulses are starchy and tend to create foam when they cook – this starchy foam can block the pressure cooker vents. Making sure you don't overfill your cooker and adding oil will help keep the foam at bay.

If you find that your beans and pulses are taking longer than they should, there are two possible reasons. Firstly, they might be old stock. Try to make sure that you buy any dried products from somewhere with a high turnover of stock and check the date. If you don't think you will need them for a while, it is possible to freeze them – this will preserve their freshness. You can also soak them and then freeze them, which has the added benefit of shaving another couple of minutes off the cooking time.

The second possible reason is water. Many of us live in areas with very hard water, which beans and pulses do not like as it inhibits the softening process. So, if at all possible, cook them in filtered water. It will make a difference.

Finally, contrary to popular opinion, I find it is better to add a little salt right at the beginning. Half a teaspoon is more than enough.

Black Beans

This is a version of the meal my sister-in-law cooked for me that first opened my eyes to the virtues of pressure cooking. It was an extremely simplified version of Brazil's national dish, *Feijoada*, in which she cooked the beans by themselves and at the same time fried bacon pieces and sausages, which she added to the beans at the end. It's quite amazing how quickly the beans take on the flavours of the meat.

This is a vegetarian dish, but I have given a meat version in the variations below. I also like to simmer some greens in the dish towards the end. This dish also makes a good soup – I purée half, and leave some beans whole for texture.

500g black beans, soaked or unsoaked

2 bay leaves

1 head of garlic, cloves separated and 2 finely chopped

2 tsp ground cumin

1 tsp dried oregano

Small bunch of coriander, leaves and stems separated, both finely chopped

1 tbsp vegetable oil

1 red onion, cut lengthways into wedges

1 tbsp olive oil

3 medium tomatoes, chopped

Juice of 1 lime

2 tsp sherry

Salt and freshly ground pepper

Put the beans, bay leaves, whole garlic cloves, cumin, oregano and coriander stems in the pressure cooker and add enough water that the tops of the beans are covered by 2cm. Add the vegetable oil, close the lid and bring to high pressure. Cook the beans for 12 minutes if you have soaked them, or for 22–25 minutes if you haven't. Allow to release pressure naturally.

When the beans are cooked, drain them, reserving around 300ml of the cooking liquid. Return the beans and the reserved liquid to the pressure cooker. Season well with salt and black pepper.

While the beans are cooking, fry the red onion in the olive oil until it is soft and brown around the edges. Add the chopped garlic and sauté for another minute. Add the tomatoes and allow to cook for a minute until starting to break down, then pour the mixture into the beans. Simmer over a low heat, then add the lime juice, sherry and coriander leaves. Check once more for seasoning and serve.

Variations

Simple *Feijoada*

Follow the instructions for cooking the beans. Meanwhile, fry the red onion along with 100g bacon lardons and 100g chopped spicy chorizo (ideally Portuguese). When the onion has softened and the bacon is crisp and brown, remove from the frying pan and add 450g sausages (about eight). You shouldn't need to add more oil, as some of the bacon fat will have been released. When the sausages are cooked, remove from the pan and add the tomatoes – use them to deglaze the frying pan, allowing them to bubble up while you scrape off any bits stuck on the bottom of the cooker. Drain the beans and return them to the cooker, along with the reserved liquid and seasoning as in the main recipe, then add the onion, bacon, chorizo and tomatoes. Cut the sausages into chunks and add them too. Proceed as before.

Vegetarian chilli

Turning this into a chilli is simple, as most of the flavours are already there. Simply add more vegetables when frying the red onion, along with some fresh chillies and more garlic. Interrupt the cooking of the beans 5 minutes before the end and add this mixture, along with some cayenne pepper and some chipotle, if you have it, for smokiness. I also add a couple of squares of dark chocolate for extra depth and richness. Serve with grated cheese, chopped avocado, lime wedges and raw onion.

Boston Baked Beans

My mother used to cook this regularly in the winter and would add pork, bacon and sausage, along with vegetables such as carrot and small onions. If you want to do the same, I suggest frying the sausages (and button onions) separately, and interrupting the cooking time to add them and any other vegetables 5 minutes before the end.

500g dried haricot beans, soaked or unsoaked

2 tbsp vegetable oil

200g belly pork or shoulder, cut into chunks

50g smoked bacon, cut into lardons

1 onion, sliced

2 garlic cloves, finely chopped

4 cloves

2 spokes of star anise

1 tsp allspice berries

1 mace blade

2 bay leaves

1 thyme sprig

1 curly parsley sprig

400g tin of chopped tomatoes

100ml red wine

1 tbsp Dijon mustard

3 tbsp black treacle

Salt and freshly ground pepper

Put the beans in the pressure cooker. Cover with water so it comes to around 2cm above the top of the beans. Add 1 tablespoon of the vegetable oil and ½ teaspoon of salt. Close the lid, bring to high pressure, then cook for 5 minutes if soaked, 15 minutes if unsoaked. Fast release.

Drain the beans in a colander and set aside, reserving the cooking liquid. Heat the remaining tablespoon of vegetable oil in the pressure cooker. Fry the belly pork and the bacon over a high heat until crisp, brown and releasing some fat. Add the onion and garlic and fry for a further minute.

Put all the herbs and spices into a square of muslin and tie into a bag (for easy removal later). Add this bag to the pressure cooker, along with the tomatoes. Return the beans to the pressure cooker. Pour the red wine into the empty tomato tin, then top up with some of the reserved cooking liquid. Add this and another tinful of the cooking liquid to the pressure cooker, then add the mustard and treacle. Season with black pepper only at this stage.

Close the lid and bring to high pressure. Cook for 5 minutes for soaked beans, 10 minutes for unsoaked, then allow to drop pressure naturally. The beans should be cooked through but not in the slightest bit mushy. Taste and add more black treacle or seasoning if you feel it needs it. Leave to simmer gently just to thicken the sauce.

Vegetable Baked Beans

This recipe came about because I wanted to develop a healthy, vegetable-rich version of baked beans that the children would like as much as the tinned, processed variety. It is particularly useful if you have a child who doesn't normally like vegetables, as here they are hidden away. You can vary the vegetables as much as you like, for example by substituting the sweet potato with butternut squash, but please try to include the celery and mushrooms – they really help to develop the savoury (umami) flavours. I have given you a double amount here, as the whole point of baked beans is that they should be a convenience food. I make a big batch and freeze in small Tupperware containers for quick and easy meals.

500g dried haricot beans, soaked or unsoaked
2 tbsp vegetable oil
½ tsp salt
1 onion, studded with 4 cloves
2 bay leaves
1 thyme sprig
1 rosemary sprig
4 garlic cloves, left unpeeled

For the sauce
3 tbsp olive oil
2 onions, roughly chopped
2 celery sticks, roughly chopped
2 carrots, roughly chopped
6 mushrooms, roughly chopped

1 sweet potato, roughly chopped
2 garlic cloves, finely chopped
400g tin of chopped tomatoes
1 tsp Marmite or other yeast extract
1 tsp treacle (optional)
Salt and freshly ground pepper

First, cook the beans. Put them in the pressure cooker and add cold water up to the halfway mark on the inside of your cooker. Add the oil and salt. Tie the onion, herbs and garlic into a loose muslin bag and add this too. Close the lid, bring to high pressure and cook for 10 minutes if soaked, 22 minutes if not. Allow to drop pressure naturally.

Strain the beans, reserving one ladleful of the cooking liquor. Wipe the inside of the pressure cooker and add the olive oil. Heat to quite a high temperature, then add all the vegetables and garlic. Cook very briskly for a few minutes until they start to brown. Pour over the tomatoes, swill out the tin with the reserved bean liquor and add to the pressure cooker. Stir in the Marmite. Close the lid, bring to high pressure and cook for 4 minutes, then fast release.

Purée until smooth (I push through a sieve just to make sure). Taste and adjust the seasoning – if you want it sweeter, add the treacle, but I don't tend to think it's necessary. Return the beans to the pot and gently stir to combine.

Fresh Borlotti Beans

During the summer, the markets across Europe are piled high with beautiful, fresh borlotti beans, unpodded and ranging from a vibrant cerise when at their freshest to a wrinkled *café au lait* when they start to dry out. Until recently, they were not so easy to find here in the UK, but I've noticed now that a lot of people are growing them alongside the more traditional runner bean, not only because they look so beautiful, but because they have such a wonderfully creamy flavour.

In winter I like to pair dried borlotti beans with bitter Italian greens such as *cime di rapa* or escarole. These aren't available in the summer, so I use chard or perhaps rocket instead. You can omit them altogether and just serve the beans with lots of soft, buttery courgettes. I also like to break up some burrata cheese or very soft, fresh mozzarella over the beans, just before serving.

250g fresh borlotti beans, or around 125g dried beans

100ml white wine

1 head of garlic, separated into unpeeled cloves

1 savory sprig if you can get it, otherwise flat-leaf parsley

2 tbsp olive oil

1 large courgette, cut diagonally in thick slices

Bunch of Swiss chard, *cime di rapa*, escarole or rocket

Squeeze of lemon juice

2 large tomatoes, green core removed, chopped

1 red onion, cut lengthways

into small wedges

1 carrot, very thinly sliced

100g runner beans, sliced

Bunch of basil, roughly torn

50g Parmesan, grated

Salt and freshly ground pepper

Extra virgin olive oil, to serve

Put the borlotti beans in the pressure cooker. If you are cooking fresh or soaked dried beans, cover with at least 2cm of water and add the white wine, garlic cloves and savory or parsley. Cook for 8 minutes if fresh, a scant 10 minutes if soaked. If you are using unsoaked dried beans, cook at high pressure for 20 minutes, then fast release, add the wine, garlic and herbs and cook at high pressure for a further 8–12 minutes.

Meanwhile, heat the olive oil in a frying pan. Over a medium heat, briskly fry the courgette until still firm but browned on all sides. If you are using Swiss chard, cut the stems into 1cm slices, squeeze lemon juice over them and fry alongside the courgettes.

Strain the borlotti beans, reserving 200ml of the cooking liquor. Return the beans and reserved liquid to the pressure cooker. Add all the vegetables, then season with salt and pepper, close the lid and bring to high pressure. As soon as high pressure is reached, remove from the heat and allow to drop pressure naturally. Stir in the basil and the Parmesan. Serve with a glug of extra virgin olive oil.

Greek 'Gigantes' (Big Beans)

Finding a successful method for cooking these beans has been a huge challenge, but I was determined to get it right, as it's one of my favourite meze dishes. Butter beans are notoriously difficult, even when cooked conventionally: there seems to be a very small window between too hard and complete mushy disintegration. Part of the problem is undoubtedly the quality of the beans available, as many of them are too old, but it's also that they do need careful cooking. Touch wood, the method below has never yet failed, and has also solved another problem I have sometimes had with these beans – that they can taste unpleasantly bitter.

I based this recipe on a dish I had in a tavern in the tiny mountainous village of Castagna, a short distance from my parents' house in Greece. It is renowned for its grilled meats, but I found their beans to be the best I have tasted anywhere. Their secret is to make the tomato sauce with stock.

250g unsoaked butter beans
4 tbsp olive oil
1 tsp salt

For the sauce
2 tbsp olive oil
1 onion, finely chopped

2 carrots, cut into 1cm rounds
¼ fennel bulb, chopped
4 garlic cloves, finely chopped
250ml chicken, vegetable or lamb stock

3 ripe tomatoes, peeled, seeded and chopped (or 150g tinned)
2 tbsp very finely chopped parsley, plus more to garnish
1 tsp ouzo (optional)
Salt and freshly ground pepper

First, cook the beans. Rinse them under cold water, then put in the pressure cooker and cover with water – do not let it rise above the halfway mark. Add 2 tablespoons of the oil and ½ teaspoon of the salt. Close the lid, bring to high pressure, then cook for 2 minutes only. Fast release.

Drain the beans, discarding any small, wrinkly floaters. Cover again with cold water and add the rest of the oil and salt. This time, bring to medium pressure, cook for 5 minutes and allow to release pressure naturally. Drain the beans again – they should now be cooked. Set aside until needed.

For the sauce, heat the olive oil in the pressure cooker and add the onion, carrots, fennel and garlic. Sauté for a couple of minutes, then add the stock. Allow this to boil and bubble furiously until you have reduced it by about half, then add the tomatoes and parsley. Season well, then return the beans to the pressure cooker. Close the lid, bring back to high pressure and cook for 1 minute only, again allowing to release pressure naturally. Add the ouzo if you like. Serve with more finely chopped parsley.

Garbure

Garbure is a thick, bean-based *potage* from south-west France (the other of course being cassoulet). It's traditionally made at the end of winter to use all those vegetables that you might still have to hand at that time of year – turnips, cabbages, carrots, potatoes. The key is to cook the vegetables until they are very soft and starting to break down in the liquid, then leave to stand for a while, preferably overnight, so that the flavours all combine well. Garbure will usually include some kind of meat – bacon, ham, particularly duck or goose confit and/or perhaps some kind of sausage. If you happen to have confit duck legs, or want to make some, use three or four of those, otherwise follow this recipe for the next best thing. The salt marinade is not essential, but will make the duck taste more like a traditional confit. If you can, use a combination of duck stock and water in which to cook the beans. You could also simply add a duck carcass to the pressure cooker or use chicken stock.

500g French garlic boiling sausage (optional)	1 litre duck or chicken stock and/or water	**For the marinated duck**
300g cannellini beans, soaked or unsoaked	1 duck carcass (optional)	3–4 duck legs
2 medium onions, sliced	1 tbsp olive oil	2 tsp thyme leaves
8 garlic cloves, 4 chopped, 4 left unpeeled	2 leeks, cut into chunks	½ tsp dried oregano
Bouquet garni (see page 16) of thyme, parsley, 2 bay leaves, 2 cloves, ½ tsp allspice berries and 1 tsp black peppercorns	2 turnips, cut into eighths	4 garlic cloves, crushed
	4 carrots, cut into 2cm rounds	1 bay leaf, crumbled
	3 floury potatoes, sliced	3 tbsp salt
	1 cabbage (preferably savoy or green), cut into wedges	½ tsp black peppercorns
	Salt and freshly ground pepper	

Unless you are using ready-made confit duck legs, begin by marinating the duck. Crush the thyme leaves, oregano, garlic, bay leaf, salt and peppercorns in a pestle and mortar, otherwise blitz in a food processor. Rub this mixture over the duck legs, including the cut sides, and put in the fridge for as long as possible, but for at least a couple of hours.

If you are using the sausage, you can either boil it for 5 minutes in the pressure cooker before you start cooking the beans, or you can boil it conventionally for 15 minutes.

Put the beans in the pressure cooker, add one of the onions, the unpeeled garlic cloves and the bouquet garni. Pour over the stock and/or water and, if you are using it, break up the duck carcass and tuck it in amongst the beans. Close the lid, bring to high pressure and cook for 28 minutes. Fast release.

When the beans are nearly finished cooking, deal with the duck. Rinse off the salt mixture and pat dry. Heat 1 tablespoon of olive oil in a large frying pan and fry the duck legs until they are well browned and have released much of their fat. Remove from the pan and pour off most of the duck fat. Add all the vegetables to the pan, including the remaining onion, garlic and the cabbage wedges, and quickly brown them over a high heat. You may have to do this in batches.

When the beans have finished cooking, remove the carcass if used, then add all the vegetables, duck legs and sausage to the pressure cooker. Deglaze the frying pan with a little of the cooking liquor, allowing it to bubble up while you scrape off any bits stuck on the bottom of the pan, and pour back over the beans. Check for seasoning, adding salt and pepper as needed. Close the lid and bring to high pressure again. Cook for another 3 minutes, then allow to release pressure naturally. Remove the duck legs, pull them apart and return the meat to the pressure cooker. Keep simmering until you are ready to serve. The *potage* should be thickened by the potatoes, but should not be too mushy.

One-pot Lentils with Sausages

One of my favourite combinations, this recipe can be varied hugely – I add spices such as cumin and a touch of cinnamon to the lentils if cooking with a Merguez or other lamb sausage, or I use rosemary and lemon in place of the fennel and parsley. If you want a simple vegetarian version of braised lentils, which is very versatile as a side dish, simply omit the sausages. It may seem odd to be cooking the lentils for a different amount of time to the Puy lentil recipe on page 135, but they do take much longer in this braise.

---

1 tbsp olive oil
8 herby sausages (I like Toulouse or fennel-flavoured Italian sausages)
1 onion, finely diced
1 leek, finely diced
1 carrot, finely diced

1 celery stick, finely diced
½ fennel bulb (optional), finely diced
100ml red wine
2 garlic cloves, finely chopped
1 tsp fennel seed
1 bay leaf

1 tbsp finely chopped flat-leaf parsley
200g green or brown lentils (I normally use Puy)
300ml water or stock (chicken, pork or ham is good)

Heat the oil in the pressure cooker. Quickly brown the sausages on all sides, then remove. Add the onion, leek, carrot, celery and fennel and fry until they have taken on some colour. Pour in the wine and allow it to bubble furiously so that it deglazes the base of the pressure cooker and until it has reduced by at least half.

Add the garlic, fennel seed and herbs, then stir in the lentils. Pour in the water or stock and return the sausages to the cooker. Close the lid and bring to high pressure. Cook for 7 minutes, then allow to reduce pressure naturally. Test for doneness: if the lentils are still a little hard, simmer for a few more minutes before serving.

Chickpeas with Chorizo, Black Pudding and Cabbage

This is a sweet, spicy stew for cold winter days. It is almost impossible to overcook chickpeas. They always stay firm enough when added to curries and soups and still absorb flavour. I always keep some ready-cooked. I cook 500g at a time and keep them in the freezer so that I can add handfuls to anything that needs bulking out – or simply to make a quick salad. They are especially good warmed through with garlic, spinach and lemon and served with some slices of sausage.

If cooking unsoaked chickpeas, I would suggest 28–32 minutes at high pressure is sufficient, depending on how much more cooking time they will get in the respective recipe, but no harm will be done if you exceed this a bit. Soaked chickpeas need more care. Cook for no more than 20 minutes, 18 should suffice.

250g chickpeas, soaked or unsoaked
1 bay leaf
1 tbsp vegetable oil
1 tsp olive oil
2 spicy cooking chorizos, sliced on the diagonal
8 small black puddings or morcilla
1 large red onion, sliced lengthways into wedges
½ white cabbage, thickly sliced
1 eating apple, peeled and sliced
2 garlic cloves, finely chopped
1 tsp fennel seed
Pinch of ground cloves
Pinch of ground allspice
½ tsp hot paprika
50ml cider or apple juice
Salt and freshly ground pepper
Chopped flat-leaf parsley, to garnish

First cook the chickpeas. Put them in the pressure cooker with the bay leaf and ½ teaspoon of salt. Add the water to the halfway mark, pour in the vegetable oil and close the lid. Bring to high pressure and cook for 20 minutes if soaked, 32 minutes if not. Allow to drop pressure naturally.

Meanwhile, heat the olive oil in a frying pan and add the cooking chorizo. Fry on both sides, then remove and fry the black puddings. Remove these too, and drain off most of the fat that will have been released from the chorizo. Return the frying pan to the heat and quickly fry the red onion and white cabbage, until they start to take on colour but retain their bite. Finally, fry the eating apple for 3 minutes and reserve.

When the chickpeas have finished cooking, drain, reserving the cooking liquor, and return to the pressure cooker. Add everything else to the pressure cooker, including the reserved cooking liquor, except for the black puddings and apple. Season. Bring to high pressure for 2 minutes only, then fast release. Add the black puddings and apple, then simmer for a minute or two. Serve in large bowls with a sprinkling of chopped parsley.

Puy Lentil Salads

These are small, green-flecked lentils with a nutty, sometimes peppery, flavour. Their firm texture makes them extremely versatile. I use them in salads or as a warm side dish with game, duck or, best of all, sausages. Other green or brown lentils may require slightly less cooking.

To cook, rinse your lentils in a sieve, then put in the pressure cooker (allow roughly 30g per person) and cover with 2cm water – you don't have to measure this as you will be draining them anyway. Do not forget to add a tablespoon of oil! Close the lid and bring to high pressure. Cook for 1 minute only, then leave to drop pressure naturally. Your lentils should be perfectly *al dente*. Here are some suggestions for using them in salads:

1. Simply mix the lentils with some mustard dressing (see below), some finely chopped shallot or onion and lots of fresh herbs – I like a mixture of flat-leaf parsley, chervil and basil and perhaps some sorrel leaves. This is a good basic salad to keep in the fridge for snacking on – and to add other things to, such as cherry tomatoes.

2. Add to the Warm Beetroot and Carrot Salad with Smoked Mackerel (see page 181), to make it more substantial.

3. Mix the lentils and mustard dressing (see below) with ribbons of smoked duck breast or fried bacon lardons, and pile into endive leaves. You could also top these with fried quail eggs.

4. Make the fennel 'confit' on page 174. Mix with some segments of orange, some crumbled goat's cheese, lots of chopped parsley or mint, and the mustard dressing.

5. One to do when you have a glut of runner beans and pigeons are at their cheapest: cook some shredded runner beans in the pressure cooker – put them in 50ml water, cook for 1 minute only at high pressure and fast release. Serve with lentils, pot-roasted and seared pigeon or partridge breasts and a herby dressing.

Mustard Dressing

1 tbsp mustard (preferably Dijon)	1 garlic clove, crushed	6 tbsp oil – groundnut, olive and walnut are all very good
1 tsp honey	2 tbsp cider vinegar	Salt and freshly ground pepper

Simply whisk all the ingredients together and season with salt and pepper to taste. Add a little water if you feel it needs thinning out.

Black Eyed Peas with Vegetables

This is very much a storecupboard/freezer concoction, handy for those times when you don't have much else around. I throw in anything that is available – carrots at the start, courgettes at the end.

2 tbsp olive oil
1 small onion, finely chopped
2 garlic cloves, finely chopped
1 tsp ground cumin
1 large pinch turmeric
½ tsp nigella seeds (onion seeds)

200g dried black eyed peas
1 bay leaf
1 sachet creamed coconut
500ml water or stock
Salt and freshly ground black pepper

3tbsp coriander stems, finely chopped
150g frozen peas or petit pois
150g frozen spinach
Juice of half a lime
A few coriander leaves

Heat the olive oil in the pressure cooker. Add the onions and sauté for 2 minutes. Add the garlic and spices and sauté for a further minute. Add the black eyed peas, creamed coconut and bay leaf then cover with the water or stock. Season with ½ tsp salt and a few grindings of black pepper.

Close the lid and bring to high pressure. Cook for 9 minutes at high pressure, then fast release. Check the black eyed peas – they should be almost done, quite *al dente*. Add the coriander stems, still frozen peas and spinach, close the lid and bring to high pressure again. Cook for a further 2 minutes, then fast release again.

Check for seasoning – you will probably need more salt at this stage. Add the lime juice, sprinkle with coriander leaves and serve.

Dhal

When I first wrote about pressure cookers, it was the fact that you can cook certain types of dhal in less than 5 minutes that seemed to excite people the most. There is a seemingly inexhaustible list of different lentils and what to do with them. Here is a handful of my favourites. You will notice that the first two, at least, are very simple in terms of ingredients – this is because I serve them more as accompaniments, so want something creamy and soothing, not packing a punch. The last recipe I'm happy to eat on its own, with some naan or chapati.

I use the same 'tempering' (oil, cumin and onion mix) and garnishes for all my dhals. It isn't necessary to always include the cumin, I do so purely because it's my favourite spice. You could use some curry leaves here, too.

Whole Dhal – Moong or Urud

This is a very dense, nutty, wholesome dhal. My mother-in-law insists that urud dhal, whether whole or the split white lentils (see page 139), must be cooked with ginger to counteract any stomach problems it might cause! She also recommends soaking for 15 minutes, but I only bother with this when she is peering over my shoulder!

250g urud lentils	Salt	**For the 'temper'**
4 garlic cloves, chopped	Coriander leaves, to garnish	Vegetable oil or ghee
2cm piece of root ginger, grated	Sliced green chillies, to garnish (optional)	1 tsp cumin seed
1 tsp turmeric	1 lemon, cut into wedges, to serve	1 onion, sliced
1 tsp chilli powder		

Wash the lentils and put in the pressure cooker with the garlic, ginger, turmeric and chilli powder. Pour over 1 litre of water. Close the lid, bring to high pressure and cook for 12 minutes. Release pressure naturally.

Meanwhile make the 'temper'. Heat a 3mm layer of oil or ghee in a frying pan. Add the cumin seed and fry until it starts to splutter, then add the onion. Fry until it is soft and brown. Pour the onion and cumin mixture into the cooked lentils and add salt to taste. Simmer until thick. Serve with coriander leaves, some sliced green chillies if you want extra heat, and wedges of lemon for squeezing.

White Lentils

This is made with white urud lentils – the same lentils as for the previous Whole Dhal recipe but split and with the skins removed. I don't think you can get a simpler dish than this – it could almost be temple food with its firm texture and clean, fresh taste. I make it regularly, as it's my husband's favourite, and we often eat it instead of rice. You can also add turmeric and garlic, if you like.

250g white urud lentils
5cm piece of root ginger
1 tbsp vegetable oil
Salt

Coriander leaves, to garnish
Sliced green chillies,
  to garnish (optional)

For the 'temper'
Vegetable oil or ghee
1 tsp cumin seed
1 onion, sliced

Wash the lentils thoroughly until they become less starchy. Put them in the pressure cooker and cover with 375ml water (the ratio is 1:1½ with these lentils). Grate the ginger directly over the lentils so that you catch all the juice. Add the oil and ¼ teaspoon of salt. Close the lid and cook at high pressure for 5 minutes, then release naturally.

Make the 'temper' as described in the Whole Dhal recipe (see page 137). Pour into the cooked lentils, add salt to taste and simmer until thick. Garnish with fresh coriander and green chillies if you want extra heat.

Channa (Red Lentil) Dhal

This is my favourite dhal. It has been a discipline writing this one down, as I usually add a bit of this, a bit of that, so it is never the same twice. I also tend to use mainly whole spices for this one, although I always grind fenugreek as it is hard to spot amongst the dhal and is bitter if you get a direct hit. You can use the same amount of ground fenugreek if you prefer. Instead of the spice blend, feel free to use a good-quality masala/curry powder.

1 tbsp vegetable oil
1 onion, chopped
2 garlic cloves, finely chopped
2cm piece of root ginger,
  finely chopped
300g red lentils or channa
  dhal, well rinsed
2 tbsp chopped coriander
  stems
200g tinned chopped tomatoes
Salt
Coriander leaves, to garnish

Sliced green chillies,
  to garnish (optional)
1 lemon, cut into wedges,
  to serve

For the spice blend
5cm piece of cinnamon stick
4 cloves
4 green cardamom pods
2 black cardamom pods
1 mace blade
1 tsp coriander seed

1 tsp cumin seed
1 tsp fenugreek seed, ground
½ tsp nigella seed
½ tsp black peppercorns
½ tsp turmeric
½ tsp cayenne pepper

For the 'temper'
Vegetable oil or ghee
1 tsp cumin seed
1 onion, sliced

Heat the vegetable oil in the pressure cooker. Add all the ingredients for the spice blend and fry until they start to splutter and smell aromatic. Add the chopped onion, garlic and ginger and continue to fry until everything has started to turn a light golden brown.

Stir in the lentils and the coriander stems, add a generous pinch of salt and pour over 750ml water and the tomatoes. Close the lid and bring to high pressure. Cook for 1 minute only, then leave to release pressure naturally. Alternatively, cook for 5 minutes and fast release.

Stir thoroughly as much of the dhal will be sitting on the top. Make the 'temper' as described in the Whole Dhal recipe (see page 137). Pour into the cooked lentils, add salt to taste and simmer until thick. Garnish with fresh coriander, green chillies if you want extra heat and wedges of lemon for squeezing.

Variation

'Haleem'

To make a simple version of the celebratory 'haleem', you can add lamb to the above dahl. Simply fry 500g cubed lamb or mutton in butter or ghee then add all the remaining ingredients except the dahl garnishes and temper. Fry for a couple more minutes then add 750ml water or chicken stock. Bring up to high pressure and cook for 20 minutes. Fast release, add the red lentils and cook on high pressure for a further minute's slow release. Serve with the same garnishes and temper as before.

Rice, Grains and Pasta

'It will probably take you around 10–12 minutes from the time you start cooking to the time you get the food on the table'

If, like me, you are a busy working parent, you are likely to find this the most useful chapter in the entire book. I really care about the food I give to my children and try to make sure that the majority of what I give them is unprocessed and made from scratch – it's a constant battle managing to do this and still feed them quickly.

So I am not exaggerating when I say that the day I discovered the pressure cooker methods for pasta and rice was a life changing one! I try to be organised and keep a store of home-made food in the freezer for quick meals, but it is typical that I will have run out on the day I'm running late and have a 20-minute window to feed tired and hungry children before they go into meltdown. This is where pasta dishes particularly come into their own. It will probably take you around 10–12 minutes from the time you start cooking to the time you get the food on the table, something I find miraculous, particularly when you consider that it can sometimes take that long simply to get enough water boiled in which to cook the pasta!

It's a similar story with most of my rice dishes. The spelt and barley risotto recipes (see pages 158–9) take slightly longer, but not much – you will have something to eat within 25–30 minutes. All the recipes are infinitely adaptable; just follow the basic timings and make sure you use the specified ratios of grain to liquid and you won't go wrong.

There are plenty of other grains that don't feature in recipes in this chapter. However, as they are useful additions to all kinds of dishes, I have included some general cooking instructions and tips.

One-pot Pasta

I didn't quite believe it when I first discovered how quickly it's possible to make an all-in-one pasta dish from scratch in the pressure cooker. The dried pasta is cooked in water and the sauce ingredients – it's an absorption method used sometimes in Italy and even more often in Spain. The benefits are clear: you are saving fuel by cooking the sauce and the pasta together, in a fraction of the time it usually takes to cook either. You are also saving water, as you don't need a huge amount in which to cook the pasta. And you are feeding hungry mouths very quickly! This method works brilliantly as long as you follow a few simple rules:

1. Be choosy about your pasta. Short pastas that generally take 8–12 minutes if cooked conventionally work best, so yes to penne, rigatoni, fusilli, macaroni. Be careful with farfalle and conchiglie (shells) – they tend to stick together so cook unevenly, and can be hard to separate. Spaghetti presents an obvious difficulty with this method, because it is too long to fit into the pressure cooker in its dry state. When I cook for the children, I break the spaghetti in half, which is a better length for them to deal with anyway. I also use those little 'nests' of tagliatelle, pappardelle and linguine, which are also available for spaghetti, but harder to find. If the pasta hasn't cooked through after 6 minutes, just add any remaining ingredients and leave to steam, covered, for a couple more minutes.

2. If you are making a sauce that contains tomatoes, do not stir once you have poured them over the other ingredients as they can inhibit cooking. One other thing I often do when making a tomato-based sauce is to add some cream cheese at the end – this helps thicken up the sauce and gives the kids a bit of extra protein. You can also bake any of the pasta recipes in the oven afterwards, with cheese sprinkled on top.

3. If you need to cook just the pasta because you already have a sauce made, you can still use this method. Simply put the pasta in the pressure cooker, season with salt and pepper, add a tablespoon of oil to help prevent foaming and almost cover with water (or stock, if you like). Cook for 6 minutes at high pressure. You should quick release, but be careful – it is possible that foam may push itself up through the valves, so it is better to fast release using the cold water method in this instance (see page 16). Pour your sauce over to heat it through, if it is the type of sauce that you want to completely combine with the pasta.

4. Finally, it is also possible to cook lasagne in the pressure cooker. Simply layer it up as normal, cook at high pressure for 25 minutes, then sprinkle with cheese and brown under a grill. I also like to make a Mexican lasagne this way, layering up tomato sauce, black bean chilli, sweetcorn, crème fraîche, cheese and tortillas, one of the most moreish things I've ever eaten.

Basic Tomato Pasta

I often add a pinch of ground cinnamon to tomato sauces – it helps bring sweetness to the sauce without having to add sugar. See below for other things you can add.

2 tbsp olive oil

1 onion, very finely chopped

3 garlic cloves, finely chopped

1 thyme sprig

Pinch of ground cinnamon

250g dried short pasta (see page 143)

400g tin of chopped tomatoes

100g cream cheese (optional)

Salt and freshly ground pepper

Coat the base of the pressure cooker with olive oil. Cook the onion and garlic over a low heat until softened then add the thyme and cinnamon. Add the dried pasta, pour over the tomatoes, then rinse the tin out with water and pour this over too. Remember not to stir again now that the tomatoes have been added. Add enough water that the pasta is almost, but not quite, covered. Season generously with salt and black pepper.

Close the lid, bring up to high pressure and cook for 6 minutes. Release pressure quickly, then stir everything together, adding the cream cheese, if using. Rest for around 3 minutes, loosely covered, just to let the flavours settle.

Other things to add

Chilli flakes

Meatballs (sausagemeat or otherwise, fried before the onion, removed and placed on top of the pasta before cooking at pressure).

Shrimp (fried before the onion and returned to the cooker after the pasta has cooked. If you have time, use the shells to make a quick stock for adding flavour). Good with fennel.

Vegetables (fine dice of whatever you have, such as carrots, celery, courgettes and squash, fried at the beginning with the onion – some will keep their shape, some will disintegrate into the sauce).

Picante chorizo (fried with onion and garlic, hot and sweet paprika, and red wine). A nod to Spain!

Pasta with Swiss Chard and Rosé Veal Meatballs

I must admit here to not always making the meatballs – I have bought rosé veal meatballs when they are reduced at the supermarket. Pork would work equally well. If you want to make your own, simply flavour some mince with lemon zest, finely chopped herbs and seasoning and shape into balls of around 4cm diameter. You could also replace the Swiss chard with spinach – just wilt in the leaves after the pasta has been cooked.

Large bunch of Swiss chard
1 tbsp olive oil
25g butter
400g rosé veal meatballs
2 garlic cloves, finely chopped

Grated zest of 1 lemon
150ml white wine
250g dried short pasta
 (see page 143)
Veal or chicken stock, or water

25g Parmesan, finely grated
100g cream cheese
Salt and freshly ground pepper

Cut the Swiss chard leaves away from the stems, chop the stems into 1cm strips and shred the leaves. Keep separate.

Heat the oil and butter in the pressure cooker and fry the meatballs so they are well browned on all sides. Remove from the cooker and add the chard stems. Sauté them for a couple of minutes, then add the garlic and cook for a minute longer. Add the lemon zest, then pour over the white wine and simmer until reduced by about half. Add the chard leaves and the pasta and stir to combine. Pour in the stock and/or water so that the pasta is almost covered and season well with salt and pepper. Put the meatballs on top.

Close the lid, bring up to high pressure and cook for 6 minutes. Release pressure quickly. Sprinkle in the Parmesan and stir in the cream cheese until thoroughly combined with the liquid – be careful as you don't want to break up the meatballs. Leave to rest for around 3 minutes, loosely covered.

Mushroom and Sage Pasta

For a non-vegetarian version, add some smoked bacon at the beginning with the mushrooms and onion, or some leftover game meat at the end – especially good if you cook the pasta in a strong game stock instead of water.

25g dried mushrooms (optional)
1 tbsp olive oil
50g butter
200g mushrooms, sliced

1 small onion, finely chopped
3 garlic cloves, finely chopped
2 tsp dried sage
50ml wine (red or white)

250g dried pasta (I favour pappardelle for this dish)
25g Parmesan
100ml cream
Salt and freshly ground pepper

If you are using the dried mushrooms, rehydrate them in a little water, as per the packet instructions. Drain them, reserving the soaking water, then roughly chop.

Heat the butter and olive oil in the pressure cooker. Add the fresh and dried mushrooms and onion and fry over a medium heat until the mushrooms are cooked through and have started to release liquid. Add the garlic and sage leaves, then pour over the wine. Allow to boil briskly (you want to cook most of the wine flavour out). Add the pasta and stir so that everything is well combined. Season with salt and pepper. Pour over enough water that the pasta is almost, but not quite, covered.

Close the lid, bring up to high pressure and cook for 6 minutes. Release pressure quickly, then stir in the Parmesan and cream and leave to simmer until the sauce has thickened sufficiently.

Pasta with Chicken Leftovers

This is particularly good if you have some gravy left over, as well as some stock. You could add bacon and any combination of vegetables here too, though I prefer it unadulterated, to the extent that I am unlikely to even add Parmesan. You could try this with other leftover meats – good combinations would be some shredded roast lamb with fresh mint, or rabbit with mustard and oregano. Incidentally, the same principle with leftovers can also be applied to risottos.

---

2 tbsp oil, butter or chicken fat skimmed from gravy or stock

1 onion or leek, finely chopped

150ml white wine

Leftover chicken, gravy (if you have it) and stock made from the carcass

250g dried short pasta (see page 143)

½ head of garlic, separated into unpeeled cloves

Small bunch of tarragon

Squeeze of lemon juice

50ml double cream (optional)

Salt and freshly ground pepper

Heat your choice of oil/fat and gently sauté the onion or leek until soft and translucent. Pour in the white wine and allow to reduce down until it is barely there. If you have any gravy, add it now, along with the pasta, garlic and tarragon. Add chicken stock and/or water until the pasta is almost covered. Season with salt and pepper.

Close the lid, bring to high pressure and cook for 6 minutes, then fast release. Fish out the garlic cloves and squish the flesh out into the sauce. Stir in the chicken, squeeze over some lemon juice and, if you want something slightly richer, add the cream too. Loosely cover with the lid and allow to stand over a very low heat for a short while, just to allow the flavours to develop.

Risotto

It has become fashionable in recent years to talk about the meditative effects of risotto-making. Apparently, stirring away at a hot stove can lull one into a delightfully calming reverie or even help you achieve mindfulness. This is all very well and good and I used to enjoy making risotto in this way myself. But the fact is that most of the time there is no chance for meditation when I have two noisy children at my heels waiting to be fed and when I'm already stressed because I need to get food on the table, fast.

No doubt some will view pressure cooker risotto to be as sacrilegious as Delia Smith's oven-baked version. All I can say is, after much experimentation, I honestly can't tell the difference between a risotto made in the pressure cooker or conventionally. It's now the only method I use – and if I want to spend some time at the stove, wooden spoon in hand, well, there's always béchamel sauce.

One word of warning: unless you are making a risotto with very strong flavours, it is best to avoid using a stock cube for these dishes – I have experimented and am yet to find one that doesn't either make the risotto too salty or give it a slightly unpleasant aftertaste. Water or a very simple vegetable stock is preferable.

I have kept the quantities of Parmesan and butter added at the end small. You can increase this considerably, depending on how rich you want your risotto to be.

Basic Risotto

1 tbsp olive oil
50g butter
1 small onion or leek, finely diced

2 garlic cloves, finely chopped
300g Arborio rice
100ml white wine
750ml stock (I favour chicken)

25g grated Parmesan, plus more to serve
Handful of basil, roughly torn
Salt and freshly ground pepper

Heat the olive oil and half the butter in the pressure cooker. Add the onion or leek and sauté gently until it is softened. Add the garlic and cook for a further minute, then stir in the rice. Keep stirring until the rice is completely covered with the oil and butter and has started to take on a glossy sheen.

Pour over the wine and turn up the heat a little. Allow the wine to bubble away until almost completely evaporated. Pour over the stock and season with salt and pepper. Close the lid and bring to full pressure. Cook for 5 minutes then release pressure quickly.

Remove the lid. Stir in the Parmesan and the rest of the butter and beat into the risotto for a couple of minutes (this is called the *mantecatura*). Loosely cover with the lid and allow to sit on a very low heat to finish cooking. Stir in the roughly torn basil just before serving and provide more Parmesan for sprinkling at the table.

Variation

Risotto alla Milanese

The traditional accompaniment to Osso Buco (page 64). Simply soak a large pinch of saffron in a little of the stock and add after the wine has evaporated. For an extra rich risotto, add chopped marrow from two beef or veal bones along with the butter at the beginning.

Sausage and Pea Risotto

This is a favourite with my children. I often replace half the peas with blanched and skinned broad beans and include some summer savory if I can get hold of it.

2 tbsp olive oil	2 garlic cloves, finely chopped	250g peas
50g butter	1 tsp dried sage or thyme	25g grated Parmesan, plus more to serve
450g pork sausages, skins removed	300g Arborio rice	
	100ml red or white wine	Salt and freshly ground pepper
1 onion, finely chopped	750ml chicken stock	

Heat 1 tablespoon of olive oil and half the butter in the pressure cooker. Cut the sausages into small lengths and fry half of them. It doesn't matter if they start to break up as they will flavour the whole risotto. Add the onion, garlic and herbs, then add the rice and proceed as for the Basic Risotto recipe (see page 149), adding the peas after the stock.

While the risotto is cooking, fry the remaining sausage pieces in the rest of the oil until crisp and brown. Add these at the end after you have beaten in the Parmesan and the rest of the butter. Serve with extra Parmesan for sprinkling.

Green Risotto

You can use any greens in this risotto – Swiss chard, spinach, even nettles if you have a good patch near you. A good garnish would be some grilled asparagus – if I was going to add this, then I'd probably make a stock from the woody ends (and some pea pods if I had them). This is a cinch to make – 2 minutes at high pressure, then strain – and will add sweetness to the risotto. Otherwise, it is up to you whether you use a vegetable or chicken stock.

Large bunch of greens – Swiss chard, spinach, nettles, rocket or even lettuce
75g butter
1 tbsp olive oil
1 onion, finely chopped

300g Arborio rice
100ml white wine
Juice of ½ lemon
750ml vegetable or chicken stock

25g grated Parmesan, plus more to serve
Grating of nutmeg
Salt and freshly ground pepper

If you are using Swiss chard, separate the stems from the leaves and finely chop both. Regardless of which greens you are using, wash them thoroughly. Do not drain too carefully – while they are still wet, throw into the pressure cooker. Bring to high pressure then switch off and release pressure immediately. Transfer the greens to a food processor and purée, adding salt and pepper, and a little more water or a squeeze of lemon juice if too dry.

Heat 50g of the butter and the olive oil in the pressure cooker and add the onion. When this is softened, add the rice and proceed as for the Basic Risotto recipe (see page 149), adding the lemon juice with the stock.

When the risotto is cooked, stir in the green purée and allow to cook for a couple of minutes, before beating in the Parmesan, the remaining 25g butter and a grating of nutmeg. Finish with another dusting of nutmeg and serve with extra Parmesan for sprinkling.

Seafood Risotto with Fennel and Dill

For this, I normally make a quick stock with the shrimp heads and shells – if you want to do so, simply fry the heads and shells with finely diced onion, garlic and carrot. When everything has taken on some colour, pour over water along with any other aromatics you fancy and one tomato, and cook in the pressure cooker for 5 minutes. Strain and it's ready to use. Otherwise just use a fish, chicken or vegetable stock.

1 tbsp olive oil	300g Arborio rice	2 tbsp chopped dill
50g butter, plus more if using scallops	100ml white wine	25g grated Parmesan, plus more to serve
500g large prawns, peeled and deveined	1 tbsp ouzo or other aniseed-based spirit, plus 1 tbsp more if using scallops	4 scallops, sliced in half widthways (optional)
1 fennel bulb, cut lengthways into wedges	Juice of ½ lemon	Salt and freshly ground pepper
2 garlic cloves, finely chopped	750ml fish, chicken or vegetable stock	Chopped curly parsley, to garnish

Heat the olive oil and half the butter in the pressure cooker. As soon as the butter is foaming, add the prawns and part-cook by searing on both sides, then remove and set aside. Add the fennel and cook until it has started to caramelise. Add the garlic and cook for a further minute. Now add the rice and proceed as for the Basic Risotto recipe (see page 149), adding the ouzo and lemon juice along with the white wine. When the risotto is cooked, beat in the dill, Parmesan and the rest of the butter, then add the prawns. Cover and allow to gently steam for a couple more minutes.

If you want to add the scallops, cook these while the risotto is steaming. Heat a frying pan until very hot. Add butter and as soon as it is foaming, add the scallops. Cook for a scant minute on each side and then add the ouzo, allowing it to flame if you like. Place on top of the risotto. Serve with some chopped fresh parsley and more Parmesan for sprinkling.

Basic Steamed Rice

Cooking plain rice could not be quicker or easier in the pressure cooker and does not need quite as much water as when cooking it conventionally. You can vary the flavours here quite considerably. Try replacing all or some of the water with stock or coconut milk. Add aromatics such as garlic, ginger, lemongrass or citrus, or soak saffron in some of the water prior to cooking.

300g basmati rice   ½ tsp salt

Rinse the rice thoroughly in cold water to remove as much starch as possible. Put the rice in the pressure cooker along with 450ml water and the salt. Close the lid, bring to high pressure and cook for 3 minutes only. Remove from the heat and allow to drop pressure naturally. The rice will keep steaming and absorbing the liquid throughout this period.

Fluff up the rice with a fork and leave to steam until you are ready to serve.

Jewelled Pilau Rice

This is a slightly richer dish than plain rice as the rice and other ingredients are lightly fried in butter or oil prior to boiling. There are endless variations: here I do a sweetly scented, jewelled version that works particularly well with the Pheasant Fesenjan on page 93.

Another favourite is to fry the rice, but omit all the spices apart from black pepper and stir in lots of green herbs at the end – a combination of parsley and mint is wonderfully fresh. I often add broad beans to that version as well, skinning them and cooking them along with the rice.

I always use whole spices when I cook these pilaus – I became accustomed to eating rice in this way at my mother-in-law's house. If you do not want to risk chomping down on a piece of cinnamon bark, please feel free to put your spices in a muslin bag, or use the same amounts of ground spices and fry with the rice at the beginning. There is no need to soak the dried fruits – the pressure cooker will soften them up very well.

50g butter or vegetable oil
3cm piece of cinnamon stick
6 green cardamom pods
2 cloves
25g dried barberries

25g golden raisins
300g basmati rice
450ml water or light chicken
  or vegetable stock

Pinch of saffron, soaked
  in 2 tbsp warm water
½ tsp salt
30g nibbed pistachios
Freshly ground pepper

Heat the butter or oil in the pressure cooker. When it has melted and started to foam, add the whole spices. Fry for a minute, then add the barberries, raisins and rice. Stir until everything is well coated with the melted butter. Add the water or stock, then strain the saffron and add its soaking liquid to the cooker. Season with the salt and some pepper, then close the lid and bring to high pressure. Cook for 3 minutes, then leave to drop pressure naturally. Serve sprinkled with pistachio nibs. *(See photograph on page 74.)*

Yakni Pilau

Rather than being a side dish, this rice dish takes centre stage. Yakni basically means 'stock', and that is what the rice is cooked in, though the stock is really cooking liquor from first cooking the meat. My mother-in-law would normally use lamb, mutton or goat on the bone – chops or ribs – but feel free to use any cut you like. You could also use unfilleted chicken thighs, but cook the meat for just 10 minutes instead of the longer times given. We normally eat this with some kind of vegetable curry dish and perhaps a prawn masala, so there's a bit of sauce to go with it.

1kg meat if off the bone, 2kg if on

750ml lamb or chicken stock, or water

1 onion, thickly sliced

4 garlic cloves

2cm piece of root ginger

2 tsp black peppercorns

4 cloves

4 black cardamom pods

1 tsp green cardamom pods

3–4cm piece of cinnamon stick

2 tsp coriander seed

1 mace blade

2 bay leaves

3 tbsp plain yoghurt

400g basmati rice, well rinsed

4 eggs (optional)

Salt and freshly ground pepper

For the 'temper'

3 tbsp vegetable oil or ghee

1 tsp cumin seed

1 onion, sliced

Put the meat in the pressure cooker. Add the stock, onion, garlic and ginger, along with all the aromatics and 1 teaspoon of salt. Bring to the boil and skim off any scum or foam that collects, then close the lid. Bring to high pressure and cook for 30 minutes if the meat is on the bone, 20 minutes if it's not. Allow to drop pressure naturally.

While the meat is cooking, prepare the garnish for the finished dish. Heat the oil or ghee in a frying pan and add the cumin seed. When it starts to smell very aromatic, add the onion and fry quite briskly until a crisp golden brown. Remove from the frying pan with a slotted spoon and drain on kitchen paper. Keep any remaining oil in the frying pan.

When the meat is cooked, strain it, discarding all the aromatics but reserving the cooking liquor. Mix the meat with the yoghurt and fry in the oil left over from cooking the onion garnish, until a rich brown.

Put the rice in the pressure cooker. Measure 600ml of the meat's cooking liquor and pour this over, then season with salt and pepper. Return the meat to the pressure cooker. If you are using them, push the whole eggs, in their shells, into the liquid. Close the lid, bring to high pressure and cook for 3 minutes. Allow to drop pressure naturally then remove the lid.

Remove the eggs and peel when they are cool enough to handle. Cut in half, lengthways. Gently fork the rice, then cover and leave to stand for a few minutes longer to dry out a bit. Serve on a platter with the eggs and onion garnish.

Chinese Rice Hotpot

This recipe comes from the limited repertoire of a Chinese ex-boyfriend. His version was a bit rough and ready, so I've refined it. It also works well with chicken, pork or even game. If you have made the Chinese Spare Ribs on page 66, any leftover sauce is excellent with this dish.

300g jasmine or basmati rice, well rinsed

450ml water or stock (duck or chicken is best)

8cm piece of very fresh root ginger

3 tbsp vegetable oil

2 large duck breasts, skinned, or 8 chicken thighs

Bunch of spring onions

4 garlic cloves, finely chopped

2 tbsp soy sauce

1 tsp chilli sauce (not sweet chilli)

5 tbsp oyster sauce

3 tsp sesame oil

75ml Shaoxing rice wine (or any other Chinese rice wine)

Large bunch of Chinese greens, spring greens or sprouting broccoli

Salt and freshly ground pepper

Put the rice in the pressure cooker and pour over the stock. Grate two-thirds of the ginger and squeeze all its juices into the stock. Add a pinch of salt and 2 tablespoons of the vegetable oil. If you are using chicken thighs, fillet them and add the bones to the rice for extra flavour. Close the lid and bring to high pressure. Cook for 3 minutes only and fast release.

While the rice is cooking, put the duck or chicken in a food processor and pulse until finely chopped and sticking together. Finely chop half the spring onions and add to the processed meat along with the rest of the grated ginger, the garlic, soy and chilli sauces, 4 tablespoons of oyster sauce, 2 teaspoons of sesame oil and the rice wine. Season with pepper and combine thoroughly.

Add the duck mixture to the pressure cooker on top of the rice and pour over around 50ml water. If you have a tall trivet, put it into the pressure cooker and sit the steamer basket on it. Put the greens or broccoli in the basket. Alternatively, make sure the greens are fairly wet from washing, wrap very loosely in lightly oiled foil and place this on top of the trivet or directly onto the meat. Close the lid and bring up to pressure. Cook for 2 minutes only and leave to release naturally.

Meanwhile make the garnish. Heat the remaining tablespoon of vegetable oil and teaspoon of sesame oil together in a frying pan. Shred the rest of the spring onions and quickly fry them, then add the remaining tablespoon of oyster sauce.

This dish is best served straight from the pot. Serve the greens on top of the meat and pour the sauce over the whole thing. Hopefully the rice will be dry and will have developed a crust on the bottom.

Spelt Risotto with Red Wine and Sausages

The first time I made a spelt risotto, it was by accident. It was supposed to be a soup, but the phone rang, I forgot all about it, and after it had spent an hour uncovered over a low heat, all the liquid had evaporated and I was left with a wonderfully creamy, nutty-tasting risotto. I've since achieved equally good versions in the pressure cooker, but of course in much less time.

I often add some kind of green to this at the end – spinach will wilt down immediately and broad beans or peas take minimal cooking, so you can simmer them for the last couple of minutes just before serving. I don't add Parmesan to this particular risotto as I think it is rich enough with the sausages.

---

2 tbsp olive oil

6 large sausages (I am biased towards Lincolnshire), skinned and broken into chunks

1 small onion, finely chopped

1 leek, finely chopped

1 carrot, finely diced

4 garlic cloves, finely chopped

1 tsp dried sage

1 tsp fennel seed

250g pearled spelt, well rinsed

150ml red wine

750ml chicken or duck stock

Finely chopped parsley, to garnish

Salt and freshly ground pepper

Heat the olive oil in the base of the pressure cooker over a medium–high heat. Fry the sausage chunks so that they brown on all sides, then remove from the cooker – they should leave behind some fat.

Add the onion, leek and carrot to the pressure cooker. Fry for a couple of minutes then add the garlic, sage, fennel seed and spelt. Stir for 1–2 minutes, making sure the spelt is well coated with oil, then pour over the red wine. Allow this to bubble furiously while you deglaze the bottom of the cooker by scraping up any brown bits left by the sausage. When the wine has almost completely evaporated, return the sausages to the pressure cooker and add the stock. Season with salt and pepper.

Close the lid and bring to high pressure. Cook for 15 minutes, then fast release. If the contents of the pressure cooker are still quite soupy, simmer for a couple more minutes – the spelt should be plump but still *al dente*. When you are ready to serve, sprinkle with finely chopped parsley.

Barley Risotto with Mushrooms, Swiss Chard and Squash

A vegetarian risotto, to which I add Parmesan, as it can do with a bit of extra creaminess. You can adapt any risotto to be made using barley. Just remember the longer cooking time and that the ratio of barley to liquid is 1:4½ rather than the normal 1:3. Barley goes very well with game, so this risotto would make a good stuffing, or you could add partridge, pheasant or pigeon to the recipe – simply fry the birds right at the beginning and cook breast-side down when cooking the risotto.

1 tbsp olive oil
25g butter
1 onion or leek, finely chopped
1 carrot, finely diced
200g firm pumpkin or squash
150g mushrooms
2 tsp dried sage

2 garlic cloves, finely chopped
200g pearled barley
20g dried porcini mushrooms, soaked in 200ml warm water
700ml water or stock (chicken, vegetable and game all work well)

25g Parmesan
Bunch of Swiss chard, leaves and stems separated and sliced
Salt and freshly ground pepper

Heat the olive oil and butter in the frying pan, add the onion, carrot, pumpkin, mushrooms and Swiss chard stems, along with the sage and garlic and fry for a minute or two. Add the barley. Strain the porcini mushrooms, reserving the soaking water. Roughly chop the mushrooms and add them to the pressure cooker. Measure the soaking water, being careful to discard any sediment at the bottom and make up the amount of liquid to 900ml with stock, water or a combination of the two. Add to the cooker and season with salt and black pepper.

Close the lid and bring to high pressure. Cook for 18 minutes, then release quickly. Stir in the Parmesan and put the Swiss chard leaves on top. Loosely put the lid over the pressure cooker base and allow the chard leaves to steam over a low heat for around 3 minutes, then stir them into the risotto. The risotto should be creamy with quite a loose texture.

Other Grains

I haven't included actual recipes for any of these grains, but as I use all of them fairly interchangeably, I thought it was worth including cooking instructions. They are all excellent as the basis of or sprinkled into salads, or used as stuffings, particularly with small game birds such as partridge.

Quinoa

Rinse the quinoa several times in water to get rid of any bitterness. If you want a nuttier flavour, dry-toast the quinoa in the base of the pressure cooker, then cover in twice its volume of stock or water (therefore, if you are cooking 250g quinoa, add 500ml of liquid) and add a pinch of salt. Close the lid and cook on high pressure for 1 minute. Allow to drop pressure naturally.

Millet

Millet is something I've started using fairly recently, including it in salads in a similar way to couscous. It has a delicious, nutty flavour, is extremely digestible (babies are weaned on it in India) and is full of nutrients, so it's well worth trying.

As with quinoa, you can toast the millet if you like, for extra nuttiness. The ratio here is 1:3, so for 250g millet, add 750ml water or stock and a generous pinch of salt. Cook at high pressure for 10 minutes, and allow to drop pressure naturally. Gently fluff with a fork. I add a pinch of turmeric and a slice or two of ginger and give it to my son when he has a bad stomach.

Bulgar Wheat

Used mainly in tabbouleh, bulgar wheat is a staple in the Middle East. You cook this in a similar way to millet – use the same 1:3 grain/liquid ratio, but don't bother toasting. For the smaller bulgar wheat, cook for 8 minutes, for the coarser ground type, cook for 10. Allow to drop pressure naturally.

Brown and Wild Rice

You can use either of these in many of the recipes I give for white rice or use them in the same way as any of the grains mentioned above. They do take longer to cook though. For brown rice, the ratio of grain to liquid is 1:2 and the cooking time is 18 minutes (similar to pearled barley). Wild rice takes slightly longer (20–22 minutes) with a grain/liquid ratio of 1:4.

Vegetables

'Pressure cooker vegetables are surprisingly good. If cooked properly, their colour will remain vibrant, they will retain more vitamins and the flavour will be stronger'

Pressure cooker vegetables are surprisingly good. If cooked properly, their colour will remain vibrant, they will retain more vitamins and the flavour will be stronger. This is to the extent that one friend, a recent convert to pressure cooking, remarked to me that she had never before tasted steamed broccoli with such an intense, fresh flavour!

Many vegetables tend to be cooked, unadulterated, as side dishes. I do not include many recipes to cover this, partly because all pressure cookers come with timing charts for steaming and boiling vegetables, although until you are used to your pressure cooker I recommend that you shave off a minute from these for *al dente* vegetables. Instead, I have given much more emphasis to cooking methods such as braising and sautéing (this, incidentally, is why so much oil, butter and cream features in these recipes!).

I always steam vegetables out of preference to boiling. I find that everything cooks more evenly and avoids becoming waterlogged. And always fast release if you want your vegetables to stay fresh and crisp – this is one of the few times when I think that the cold water method (see page 16) is worth using, as it's just that bit quicker than using the built-in fast release methods on your pressure cooker. If you want your vegetables to have a softer texture (I like this particularly with peas), allow the pressure to drop naturally – this shouldn't take long.

Always use the bare minimum of water. If steaming, I put just 2–3cm in the bottom of the pressure cooker. Do not worry about the small amounts of liquid in some of the following recipes – enough moisture comes out of the butter and vegetables during the cooking process to provide all the steam necessary to build up and sustain pressure for the very short cooking periods. If you are still nervous about this, you can instead put all the ingredients in a heatproof bowl and put this on the trivet with water underneath. You will have to do this after any browning/sautéing, so the method is a bit more involved. You will also need to add a couple of minutes to the cooking time. Some pressure cooker authors prefer this method, but I honestly don't think it's necessary.

Potatoes

Potatoes are my carbohydrate of choice: I find them the most comforting food ever. They are also infinitely adaptable, which is why there are a fair few recipes here that include them.

Mashed Potatoes

I steam these in preference to boiling – if you want to boil, add a scant 150ml water to the potatoes and cook for 8 minutes instead of 10. For a garlic mash, follow the instructions on page 182 for how to roast garlic alongside the steaming potatoes.

1kg floury potatoes, such as Maris Piper or King Edward, cut into 3cm cubes	75–100g butter, cubed 50ml milk	Salt

Put the trivet in the pressure cooker and place the steamer basket on top. Fill the basket with the potatoes and sprinkle with a large pinch of salt. Put 2–3cm water in the base of the pressure cooker. Close the lid and bring to high pressure. Cook for 10 minutes, then fast release.

Remove the basket from the pressure cooker and put the potatoes through a ricer, into a bowl. Whisk in the butter with a fork, then add enough milk to get the consistency you require.

Sautéed Potatoes and Other Vegetables

The method for this recipe is adapted from Suzanne Gibbs' book on pressure cookers and works with any root vegetables that you would normally roast or sauté. I particularly like cooking skinny parsnips this way, as I have always been good at burning the thin ends of the wedges, something that never happens in the pressure cooker. These are also delicious made with duck fat or dripping instead of oil.

500g new or waxy potatoes 3 tbsp olive oil	1 tbsp butter 4 tbsp water or stock	Salt and freshly ground pepper

Scrape the potatoes if necessary, but do not peel, then cut into fairly small chunks. You can obviously leave them whole if baby new potatoes. Heat the olive oil and butter in the pressure cooker over a high heat. Add the potatoes and fry briskly for around 3 minutes, turning until all the sides are crisping and turning brown. Season with salt and pepper, then pour over the water or stock. Close the lid and bring to high pressure. Cook for 5 minutes then remove from the heat and allow to release pressure naturally.

Variations

Herby potatoes

Add your choice of herbs at the same time as the salt and pepper. You can of course vary the herbs: my favourite combinations are dried oregano with lemon zest or rosemary with whole unpeeled garlic cloves.

To turn into a delicious one-pot meal

Start by frying some sausages and onions until caramelised and well browned, then remove. Fry the potatoes, as above, in the remaining fat, perhaps including wedges of eating apple. Sprinkle with sage, layer the sausages and onions on top, add the stock (cider is also good here) and cook as before. I also occasionally add a smoked Polish sausage here, which I don't bother frying, along with some caraway seed.

Patatas bravas

Use the Fresh Tomato Sauce on page 177 but add sweet and hot paprika and a tablespoon of sherry vinegar. Reduce quite considerably, then pour over the cooked potatoes and simmer for 1 minute.

Parsnips

Peel the parsnips and cut them into batons. Follow the main recipe, but use vegetable oil or dripping instead of butter and olive oil. When you add the liquid, you might also drizzle over a tablespoon of maple syrup along with some thyme leaves.

Celeriac

Cut into chunks rather than batons. I fry these in olive oil and butter, then once they have cooked, toss them in a tablespoon of wholegrain mustard.

Onions

I mean the little button or pickling onions here, or perhaps some shallots. Brown as in the main recipe but cook for 3 minutes rather than 5 or they are liable to disintegrate.

A Kind of Tartiflette

This is a rich and luscious lunch or supper dish, just what you need on a cold winter's day for its warming, rib-sticking properties. I have given meat and vegetarian options here – bacon is included in a traditional tartiflette, but this is hardly traditional, so feel free to replace it with the dried mushrooms to give extra oomph to the savoury flavours. If you can't get Reblochon, there are plenty of other soft cheeses you can choose from.

10g dried porcini mushrooms or 100g cubed pancetta/bacon

Butter, for greasing

50ml olive oil

1 onion, finely chopped

300g assorted fresh mushrooms, sliced

4 large garlic cloves, finely chopped

750g waxy potatoes, unpeeled and thickly sliced

1 rosemary sprig, leaves picked and very finely chopped

50ml white wine

200g Reblochon cheese or similar, thick rind removed, cubed

100ml single cream (optional)

75g Gruyère cheese, coarsely grated

Salt and freshly ground pepper

If you are using the dried mushrooms, soak them in 50ml hot water. Butter a shallow, ovenproof dish.

Heat the olive oil in the base of the pressure cooker. Sauté the onion and bacon, if using, until soft and translucent. Add the fresh mushrooms and the garlic and stir over a high heat for a couple of minutes. Add the potatoes.

Strain off the rehydrated mushrooms, reserving the liquor. Finely chop and add to the pressure cooker. Sprinkle over the chopped rosemary. Pour in the wine and the reserved mushroom liquor (or 50ml stock and/or water if not using dried mushrooms), then close down the lid and bring to high pressure. Cook for 2 minutes only and fast release. Remove the potatoes and mushrooms from the pressure cooker with a slotted spoon and arrange them in the buttered dish, along with the cubes of Reblochon. Season with salt and pepper. If necessary, simmer the remaining liquor until it is syrupy, then add the cream.

Pour the cooking liquor over the contents of the dish, then sprinkle over the Gruyère. Put under a hot grill until brown and bubbling.

Cumin Spiced Potatoes

Or *Jeera Aloo*, if you like. Of all the food my mother-in-law makes, this side dish is the one I love above all others – she kindly kept me supplied right the way through my pregnancy when I constantly craved potatoes. I sometimes substitute the cumin with nigella (onion) seed and add a pinch of asafoetida too.

Vegetable oil
1 small onion, diced
1 tbsp cumin seed

500g new or waxy potatoes, sliced into 5mm-thick rounds
2 tbsp chopped tomatoes, fresh or tinned

Green chillies, sliced (optional)
Salt and freshly ground pepper
Roughly chopped fresh coriander, to garnish

Coat the bottom of the pressure cooker in a thick layer of vegetable oil and warm over a medium heat. Add the onion and cumin seed and fry until the cumin is very fragrant and the onion has started to brown around the edges. Add the potatoes and stir until they are thoroughly coated in the aromatic oil.

Pour over 4 tablespoons of water, the chopped tomatoes and green chillies, season with salt and pepper, stir again and then close the lid. Bring to high pressure and cook for 3 minutes, then remove from the heat and allow to drop pressure naturally. Serve with a liberal sprinkling of roughly chopped coriander.

Glazed Carrots

This is a luxurious way of cooking vegetables, made as a special treat. I normally cook these with just a pinch of salt and black pepper, but sometimes vary the flavour. If doing so, I fry a small amount of cumin or caraway seed in the butter before adding the carrots, or perhaps add some finely grated lemon zest or a few sprigs of tarragon when I add the water. All these flavours are quite different, but work very well with the carrots.

| 50g butter | 500g carrots, cut on the diagonal | Salt and freshly ground pepper |

Heat the butter in the pressure cooker over a low heat. Add the carrots and turn them over until they are completely covered in the melted butter. Add 50ml water and season with salt and pepper. Close the lid and bring to high pressure. Cook for 5 minutes, then release quickly.

Crushed Carrots and Swede

I love this so much that sometimes it doesn't actually get to the table – either that or I have to make double the amount. It is always part of our Christmas dinner.

| 250g carrots, cut into 2cm rounds | Knob of butter (amount optional) | Salt and freshly ground pepper |
| 250g swede, cut into small cubes | Nutmeg (optional) | |

Put the trivet in the pressure cooker. Layer the swede and carrots in the steamer basket, with the swede on the bottom. Pour 150ml water into the pressure cooker. Close the lid and bring to high pressure. Cook for 5 minutes then release quickly.

Remove the steamer from the pressure cooker and leave the vegetables to drain for a couple of minutes, with a cloth over them, until the steam subsides. Transfer to a bowl and mash. I prefer a course, crushed texture so I just use a fork – if you want a smoother texture your best bet is a ricer. Add the butter and stir in, then season with salt and pepper. Grate over a little nutmeg as well, if you like, especially if you are serving this dish with poultry.

Brussels Sprouts with Chestnuts and Bacon

This dish always features on our Christmas menu. If you want to cook the chestnuts yourself, rather than rely on the vacuum-packed variety, see pages 183–4 for the method.

25g duck or goose fat
50g bacon lardons

500g Brussels sprouts, trimmed and cut in half lengthways

75g chestnuts, cooked and peeled
50ml Marsala

Heat the fat in the pressure cooker, then add the bacon lardons. Fry briskly until crisp and browning, then throw in the Brussels sprouts. When they have also taken on some colour, roughly crumble in the chestnuts and pour over the Marsala. Close the lid, bring to high pressure and cook for 2½–3 minutes. Fast release.

Spiced Red Cabbage and Apple

Yet another Christmassy dish, but equally good with any pork or game dish that doesn't already have lots of apple flavours running through it.

1 large red cabbage, cored and shredded
1 onion, finely chopped
2 garlic cloves, finely chopped
1cm piece of root ginger, finely chopped

1 eating apple, peeled, cored and finely diced
Pinch of ground cloves
¼ tsp ground allspice
¼ tsp ground cinnamon
1 tsp crushed juniper (optional)

1 tsp chopped fresh thyme
1 tbsp brown sugar
150ml apple juice or cider
1 tbsp cider vinegar
50g butter, cut into small dice
Salt and freshly ground pepper

Simply put all the ingredients in the pressure cooker, season with salt and pepper and mix thoroughly (I use my hands). Close the lid and bring to high pressure. Cook for 2 minutes and allow to drop pressure naturally, or for 3 minutes with fast release.

Leeks Creamed with Horseradish

This is a very good dish to eat with a braised beef recipe (such as Beef Braised in Red Wine, Orange Zest and Tarragon on page 60) or an oxtail casserole (see page 25).

25g butter
2 leeks, sliced into 1cm rings

2cm horseradish, grated,
or 1 tbsp horseradish sauce
(not creamed)

1 tbsp white wine (optional)
100ml double cream
Salt and freshly ground pepper

Put the butter in the pressure cooker and heat until foaming. Add the leeks, sauté for a minute or two until well coated with the butter, then add the horseradish and season with salt and pepper. Add white wine, if using, or add 1 tablespoon of water and close the lid. Bring to high pressure and cook for 1 minute, then fast release. Pour in the cream and simmer until well amalgamated and a little reduced. You can purée this to make a sauce if you like, but I like it as is.

Braised Leeks, Peas and Little Gems

A perfect summer vegetable side dish, which I can also quite happily eat on its own, especially if I add the bacon. If you want to transform this into something a bit more wintry, substitute the Little Gems with roughly shredded savoy cabbage. When you quarter the Little Gems, try to make sure that the leaves stay attached to the base. Neither the cream nor the alcohol is essential, but they do make for a slightly richer dish.

50g butter
1 tbsp olive oil
2 leeks, cut into 2cm rounds
75g bacon or pancetta
lardons (optional)

2–3 Little Gem lettuces,
quartered lengthways
2 tbsp white wine or
Noilly Prat (optional)
250g fresh or frozen peas

50ml double cream (optional)
Salt and freshly ground pepper

Melt the butter in the base of the pressure cooker until it starts to foam, then add the olive oil. Throw in the leeks and bacon and fry until starting to go brown around the edges. Add the Little Gems and gently turn around in the butter until they also start to go brown. If using, add a couple of tablespoons of white wine or Noilly Prat to the pan and let it bubble for a minute. Otherwise, add a splash of water and do the same, then add the peas and season with salt and pepper.

Close the lid, bring to high pressure and cook for 1 minute only, then allow to drop pressure naturally. If you want to make this very rich, add the cream. Heat it through, making sure that the lettuces are well coated.

Swiss Chard and Other Greens

Swiss chard is the vegetable I prize above all others in my garden. It grows like a weed and is very versatile in cooking, due in part to the fact that it doesn't dissolve into a mush at the merest hint of heat. Sometimes I just want a big pile of it, unadorned bar a little butter and lemon juice. The key here is to make sure that the chard has just enough water clinging to its leaves once you have drained it – this will provide just the right amount of steam required to cook it. You could give all kinds of other green vegetables, such as sprouting broccoli, similar treatment here, especially those that keep their shape – use Chinese varieties and sauté a little garlic, ginger and/or chilli at the beginning of the cooking process and perhaps add some soy or oyster sauce at the end. The possibilities are endless.

1kg Swiss chard, stems and leaves separated 1 tbsp olive oil	25g butter Squeeze of lemon or lime juice	Salt and freshly ground pepper

Cut the chard stems into 2cm chunks and roughly chop the leaves.

Heat the oil and butter in the bottom of the pressure cooker. As soon as the butter starts to foam, add the chard stems and sauté for a couple of minutes. Throw in the leaves, season with salt and pepper, put the lid on and bring to high pressure. Time for 1 minute exactly, then turn off the heat. If you want your chard soft and melting, leave to drop pressure naturally. For a more *al dente* texture, fast release immediately.

Squeeze a little lemon juice over the chard and toss it around lightly. Serve straightaway.

Fennel and Broad Beans

A lovely braised dish for summer. I find it hard to resist adding splashes of alcohol to my vegetables, and particularly love aniseedy spirits with fennel. It is, of course, entirely optional. Skinning the broad beans is also a matter of personal preference. If the broad beans are young and tender, I usually leave them intact; the larger, mealier ones will be stripped. The best way to do this is to blanch them in boiling water and then plunge into ice-cold. The skins will then slip off easily.

---

2 large fennel bulbs

1 tbsp olive oil

50g butter

1 tbsp ouzo or other aniseed-based spirit (optional)

500g broad beans, blanched, podded and skinned if needed (see above)

Small bunch of mint, roughly chopped

Salt and freshly ground pepper

Prepare the fennel bulbs – trim the roots and tops (you can save these for the stockpot), but leave the fronds on. Cut into quarters lengthways but, if you can, try and make sure that everything remains attached to the base.

Heat the olive oil and butter in the bottom of the pressure cooker. Add the fennel and sauté, turning regularly until the butter has had a chance to penetrate them a little and they are taking on a golden-brown colour. Season with salt and pepper, then splash with the ouzo.

Throw in all the broad beans. Close the lid, bring to high pressure and cook for 2 minutes. Allow to drop pressure naturally. Sprinkle over the mint just prior to serving.

Caramelised Endives or Fennel

I love this unadulterated – just endives cooked in buttery juices and a scant crumbling of sage. However, sometimes I do want something a bit more, so will add Marsala and cream as well. It depends on my mood. For a more substantial dish, think about turning the cooked endives into a gratin. Do this by wrapping them in slices of ham spread with Dijon mustard. Put these in an ovenproof dish, smother in béchamel sauce, sprinkle with cheese (Cheddar is fine) and put under a hot grill until brown and bubbling. Perfect winter food.

You could also substitute endive with fennel, replacing the Marsala with white wine or something aniseedy and the sage with dill. It works equally well as the gratin suggested above, but is also lovely as a salad with orange, Puy lentils and goat's cheese (see page 135).

4–6 heads of endive, depending on size

1 tbsp olive oil

50g butter

1 tsp dried sage, crumbled

50ml Marsala (optional)

100ml double cream (optional)

Salt and freshly ground pepper

Trim the bare minimum from the base of the endives, and cut them in half lengthways, so that all the leaves are still attached to the stem. Heat the olive oil and butter in the pressure cooker. When the butter is foaming, add the endives, cut-side down. Sauté until the cut side turns golden brown and starts caramelising around the edges, then turn over and sauté the other side. This process should take between 5–10 minutes.

Sprinkle over the sage. Then it is up to you – if you want extra sweetness, pour over the Marsala (but if you're not using it, you will not need any extra water). Season with salt and pepper, close the lid and bring to high pressure. Cook for 2 minutes only, then fast release. Add the cream now if you like.

'Confit' Tomatoes

This is one to do if you want your tomatoes to have a slow-cooked effect – I make this as part of an English fry-up, or as a topping for bruschetta. You can also wrap these in foil and cook them in a similar way to the Roasted Garlic on page 182. The sugar will help the tomatoes to caramelise and take on colour, but I would only recommend adding it if they are not at their ripe or sweet best.

500g regular or cherry tomatoes
Sprinkling of sugar (optional)

50ml olive oil
A few garlic cloves

Sea salt and freshly ground pepper

If you are using large tomatoes, cut them in half and sprinkle with sugar. Heat 1 tablespoon of olive oil in a frying pan or the pressure cooker. When it is hot, fry the tomatoes, cut-side down, as quickly as possible, so that they start taking on colour almost immediately. Put them cut-side up in a heatproof dish. If you are using smaller or cherry tomatoes, leave them whole and simply put straight in the dish.

Tuck in the garlic cloves, season with salt and pepper and sprinkle with any herbs you fancy adding (such as tarragon, thyme or sage, depending on your main dish), then pour over the olive oil. Cover the dish and place on top of the trivet in the pressure cooker. Put 2–3cm of water in the pressure cooker. Close the lid and bring to high pressure. Remove from the heat immediately and fast release (not under water).

Fresh Tomato Sauce

While I love a gutsy, well-reduced tomato sauce as much as the next person, sometimes fresh tomatoes are much better when they're given the bare minimum of cooking. This recipe softens them to a sweet creaminess, which is delicious tossed lightly through some spaghetti. The idea for containing the tomato seeds and skins in muslin is to add flavour to the sauce, as much of the tomato flavour is found in the jelly surrounding the seeds. It improves the flavour enough to make the endeavour worthwhile if you have time.

1kg ripe tomatoes	½ onion, very finely chopped	Handful of basil, roughly torn
50ml olive oil	2 garlic cloves, finely chopped	Salt and freshly ground pepper

Score a cross in the base of each tomato and plunge into freshly boiled water for 30 seconds. The skins should then easily slip off. Cut the tomatoes in half and scoop out the seeds into a sieve sat over a bowl, as you will want to keep the juices. Roughly chop the halved tomatoes. Put the seeds and skins onto a piece of muslin and tie into a small parcel with string.

Coat the base of the pressure cooker generously with olive oil. Add the onion and sauté until soft and translucent. Add the garlic and continue cooking for another minute. Pour over the collected juices from the tomato seeds, then add the chopped tomatoes and the muslin parcel. Sprinkle with a little salt and pepper. Do not stir.

Close the lid and bring up to high pressure. Cook for 1 minute only, then fast release. Return to the heat and stir vigorously. Leave on a medium heat for 2 minutes to reduce slightly. Throw in a handful of roughly torn basil.

Variations

For a richer tomato sauce

A richer tomato sauce is very useful when you don't want anything with too much liquid (for instance, if you want to layer it up with aubergine for Parmigiana di melanzane) or if you want it to stand up to stronger flavours – such as chilli, anchovy, sausage or meatballs.

Use the same amount of tomatoes, or two tins. After you have fried the onion and garlic, add some red or white wine (around 150ml) and simmer over a high heat to reduce by about half. If you are using fresh tomatoes, prepare as above. Add the tomatoes to the pressure cooker with a pinch of sugar, some salt and pepper, and any herbs you might want to add (I like thyme or dried oregano with this sauce). Cook for much longer this time – 10 minutes is enough. Again, leave to simmer for a few minutes to concentrate the sauce.

To make into soup

Either of these sauces can be used as a base for a delicious soup. I tend to use the fresh tomato sauce in summer, though I add some finely chopped celery along with the onion, and I flavour it with tarragon and a light vegetable stock (500ml should be enough). I then purée, add single cream (around 100ml) and lots of chopped basil. For a more elegant serving suggestion, omit the cream from the soup. Instead, purée it with the basil and drop into the centre of your soup, followed by a few drops of a good extra virgin olive oil.

For a winter soup, use the richer sauce, adding all the stock and flavours to the pressure cooker at the same time as the tomatoes. Use vegetable or chicken stock, and a handful of red lentils or rice to act as thickener. In terms of spices, anything goes – I like to add chilli flakes, perhaps with a pinch of saffron and ginger. I also like a paprika version with a generous drop of sherry added at the end, along with some fried finely chopped chorizo as a garnish.

Caponata

I suppose you could call this a Caponata, though the slightly unconventional ingredient combination came about when I had a lot of coriander to use up – I found it made a very nice change from parsley, so I've stuck with it here. I also once added a dollop of chipotle en adobo, which added a spicy smokiness similar to that of paprika, and made the dish feel more new world than old.

This is good over pasta (you could, at a pinch, add all these ingredients to some dried pasta and enough water to almost cover and make it the one-pot way described on page 143). I like it best, however, eaten just warmed through with toasted slices of sourdough bread and some creamy fresh mozzarella.

50ml olive oil

50g tin of anchovies (30g drained weight)

1 red onion, cut lengthways into wedges

1 celery stick, cut into 2cm chunks

2 aubergines, cut into 5cm cubes

4 garlic cloves, finely chopped

Small bunch of coriander, leaves and stems separated, stems finely chopped

½ tsp each of hot and sweet paprika

100ml red wine

400g tin of chopped tomatoes

2 red peppers, cut in half lengthways, seeded and skinned (see method on page 182)

2 tbsp capers, rinsed

2 tbsp chopped green olives

Salt and freshly ground pepper

Coat the base of the pressure cooker with a thin (¼cm) layer of olive oil. Throw in the contents of the tin of anchovies, oil and all. Cook over a medium heat, breaking up the anchovies with a spoon. Add the onion, celery and aubergines and fry over a high heat until all have started to soften and brown around the edges. Add the garlic, along with the coriander stems, and fry for a minute longer, then sprinkle over both types of paprika. Pour in the red wine, allow it to bubble furiously for a minute, then add the tin of tomatoes. Swill the tin out with a couple of tablespoons of water or wine and add that to the pressure cooker too. Finally, stir in the red pepper strips, capers and olives. Check for seasoning – it is unlikely you will need salt, but black pepper might be welcome.

Close the lid and bring to high pressure. Cook for a scant 4 minutes, then fast release. Return to the heat and allow the sauce to reduce slightly, then sprinkle over the coriander leaves. This dish tastes best when it has slightly cooled.

Warm Beetroot and Carrot Salad with Smoked Mackerel

I made this salad when I was craving Scandinavian flavours. I originally wanted to add dill, but none was to be found that day, and having made it with dill since, I actually prefer it without. Verjuice adds to the sweetness, especially an English one made with crab apples. If you can't find verjuice, apple juice mixed with a teaspoon of cider vinegar works just as well.

500g beetroot (unpeeled weight – around 5 medium-sized), peeled and cut into 1cm dice

500g carrots, cut into 1cm rounds

4 tbsp verjuice, or apple juice mixed with 1 tsp cider vinegar

1 shallot, finely sliced into crescents

2 tbsp capers (optional)

2 tbsp walnut oil

1 tbsp Dijon mustard

1 tsp wholegrain mustard

4 smoked mackerel fillets (1 per person, or you can reduce this)

Arrange the beetroot in a single layer at the bottom of the pressure cooker and put the carrots on top. Pour over 2 tablespoons of the verjuice along with a splash of water. Seal the lid, bring to high pressure and cook for 5 minutes, then remove from the heat and allow to release naturally.

Strain the beetroot and carrot into a bowl. The beetroot will have retained its intense purple colour and the carrots will have gone a shade of magenta wherever they came into contact with the beetroot juice. Fold in the sliced shallot and capers, if using.

Mix together the walnut oil, mustards and remaining verjuice. Pour this over the vegetables and stir in. Flake the smoked mackerel into fairly large chunks then very lightly combine with the other ingredients – you don't want to break it up. This is best served while still slightly warm.

A Couple of Vegetable Shortcuts

Here I include a few shortcuts that should be useful to people who cook a lot. There are ideas for their use dotted throughout the book.

Roasted Garlic

Often when I am cooking something else in the pressure cooker for just a few minutes, I will do this as a treat for my husband, who is a garlic fiend. I take a square of foil, break up a head or two of garlic cloves, leaving them unpeeled, drizzle with olive oil and add any herbs I have to hand, especially rosemary. Then I fold the foil over to make a secure parcel (ensure it is leak-proof) and pop it on top of whatever else I'm cooking. Use foil if you are adding the garlic to anything that takes fairly long cooking. For anything that takes 5 minutes or less, use greaseproof paper.

When you open your parcel, you will have lovely, creamy garlic, very similar to if you had roasted it in the oven. Not only that, the olive oil will have infused with the garlic and herb flavours, so you will also have flavoured oil to use for a dressing.

I peel and mash the garlic to stir into soups, add to creamed potatoes for a mellow garlic mash, or use on bruschetta.

Variation

Other vegetable packets

It is possible to wrap all kinds of vegetables in foil and place on top of whatever you are cooking, ready to be added to the actual dish at the end. This is especially useful if you are making a stew of some sort and you don't want mushy vegetables, but also want to save time by not cooking them afterwards. Carrots work particularly well – leave them whole and they should withstand any amount of cooking time as long as they are properly encased. I also cook leeks this way, to stop them getting waterlogged.

Roasted Red Peppers or Aubergines

It's quite expensive and time consuming to roast red peppers in order to remove the skin. This pressure cooker method is very quick and, although it might not impart quite the same smoky flavour, the charring at the beginning goes some way to assuage this loss.

Put a couple of tablespoons of olive oil in the base of the pressure cooker. Heat over quite a high heat, then add as many halved red peppers as you need and fry for a furious couple of minutes, until the skin and edges have started to go dark brown in places. *(continued on page 184)*

(continued from page 182) Remove the cooker from the heat for a minute to minimise the spluttering and spitting you will get when you add a scant 50ml water, then return to the heat, close the lid and bring to high pressure. As soon as this is reached, remove from the heat and leave the pressure to drop naturally. By the time the pressure has dropped, the steam inside will have done its work and the peppers will be very easy to peel.

This method also works well with aubergines, which can also take a while to char and roast. Prick an aubergine all over with a knife tip, then proceed as for the red peppers, letting the skin go black instead of brown, and this time cooking for 3 minutes. When the aubergine is cool enough to handle, peel off the skin and leave to drain in a sieve. You can then use it for all kinds of things, including the Baba Ganoush on page 47.

Chestnuts

It's possible to buy cooked chestnuts, usually in vacuum packs, but if you want to cook your own (perhaps you have a sweet chestnut tree or simply want to make the most of their availability in autumn and winter) the pressure cooker will save you a lot of time.

Put unpeeled chestnuts in the pressure cooker. Pour over water – they should have around 5cm covering them. Add 2 teaspoons of salt. Close the lid, bring to high pressure and cook for 5 minutes for firm chestnuts (good for chopping finely and adding to stuffings) or 8 minutes for soft (good if you want to purée them or use in desserts). Allow to drop pressure naturally. Score with a sharp knife and peel off the outer husk and the papery inner skin. Your chestnuts are now ready for use.

Carrots

For very rich and caramelised carrots that are perfect for purées, increase the amount of butter to 75g, omit the water and add a pinch of salt. You can also add a large pinch of bicarbonate of soda which will help speed up the Maillard's Reaction (caramelisation process). Cook the carrots on high pressure for 20 minutes then purée. The purée will darken to a deep orange-brown – it is excellent on its own, with added cheese or as the base for a soup. Try turning it into a soup with stock or carrot juice and some tarragon, or use this method for the root vegetable soup on page 29. This is very adaptable – it works particularly well with pumpkin and squash, to which I like to add ginger, and really brings out the sweetness of parsnips.

Puddings

'There is no doubt
that it is brilliant
for old-fashioned
steamed puddings;
it works well with
lighter fare too'

When I talk to people about pressure cookers, one memory is common to many – a whistling, rattling pressure cooker filling the kitchen with steam on Christmas day, when it was used to steam the Christmas pudding. It was the same in my house – it was just about the only thing for which my mother used the pressure cooker. Fortunately, however, the pressure cooker is capable of so much more.

Apart from steaming, the main type of dessert you can do in the pressure cooker is anything that requires a *bain marie*. I offer you some examples in this chapter – clafoutis (see page 195), the Chocolate Pots on page 196 and even a rich New York-style cheesecake (see page 193). You can also adapt your favourite crème brûlée or crème caramel recipes for the pressure cooker. Individual ramekins will take only 5 minutes under pressure.

You can also poach hard orchard fruits such as quinces and pears, not just to eat as they are, but for use in pies, crumble and puddings. At the end of the chapter, I give some time-saving tips for things like *dulce de leche* – a thick caramel sauce made in a miraculous 20 minutes instead of several hours.

Finally, you can also use the pressure cooker for baking. I haven't included any cake or bread recipes because I find that most people prefer to make cakes larger than the 20cm size that most pressure cookers can comfortably fit. However, if you want to adapt any cake recipe, you can follow the advice given for steamed puddings – i.e. make sure to steam without pressure for the first 15 minutes if you are using any raising agents and then cook for another 25 minutes. You should also make sure that your cake is well covered in a double layer of greaseproof paper.

Steamed Puddings

I have included just one recipe here (Blackberry and Apple, see page 188), but you can cook any of your favourites in the pressure cooker – just remember to let them steam without pressure for the first 15 minutes, in order for the raising agents to work. I haven't included a recipe for Christmas pudding as everyone has their own favourite. All you need to know are the cooking times – steam without pressure for 15 minutes, then cook at high pressure for 2 hours. When you want to reheat the pudding on Christmas day, you will need to cook it on high pressure for a further 30 minutes.

Lemon Surprise Pudding

I couldn't resist including this pudding as it is another childhood favourite. I used to call it 'magic pudding' because I used to help make it and so would see a uniform batter transform itself into two distinct layers of sponge and sauce. We never diverged from lemon, but I have since successfully tried it with sour oranges and chocolate (replacing the ground almonds with cocoa powder) and have come up with a much richer variation here.

50g butter
100g golden caster sugar
Grated zest and juice of 2
   unwaxed lemons

2 eggs, separated
25g self-raising flour
25g ground almonds
¼ tsp almond extract

200ml milk
Cream, to serve

Butter a round 18–20cm soufflé or pie dish. Cream together the butter, sugar and lemon zest until light and fluffy. Beat the egg yolks into the creamed mixture, one at a time. Fold in the flour and almonds, then gradually pour in the milk and lemon juice. Don't worry if the mixture curdles! Whisk the egg whites until dry and stiff, then fold into the lemony batter.

Pour into the prepared soufflé dish. Cover tightly with two layers of greaseproof paper. Place in the pressure cooker on top of the upturned steamer basket. Pour water into the pressure cooker until it is just short of the top of the basket. Lock the lid and bring to full pressure. Time for 5 minutes then remove from the heat. Slow release at room temperature. Serve hot or cold, with cream.

Variation

Sticky Coffee Surprise Pudding

Put 100g chopped dates and 100ml strong coffee in the pressure cooker and cook at high pressure for 1 minute. Reserve and wash out the pressure cooker. Proceed as above, omitting the lemon and almond extract, and replacing the ground almonds with a further 25g of flour. Fold in the dates and coffee mixture along with 2 tbsp rum and 1 tsp of vanilla extract.

Blackberry and Apple Steamed Suet Pudding

Possibly my all-time favourite pudding, mainly because I absolutely adore the scent of cooked blackberries. It's a smell I look forward to all year, and I am never disappointed.

I prefer to use eating apples in this pudding as they keep their shape better than cooking apples and you need to add less sugar.

Butter, for greasing
200g self-raising flour
Pinch of salt
100g suet

80g sugar
500g eating apples, peeled and sliced
200g blackberries

Squeeze of lemon juice
Cream or custard, to serve

Butter a 1-litre pudding basin. Make the suet crust by mixing together the flour, salt, suet and 2 tablespoons of the sugar, and add enough water to make a dry, firm dough. Chill in the fridge for at least 30 minutes. Separate a quarter of the dough to use for the lid. Roll both pieces out to a thickness of around 5mm and line the basin with the larger piece of dough. Cut out a lid from the smaller piece.

Mix the apples and blackberries together and squeeze over the lemon juice. Sprinkle with the remaining sugar and pour the whole lot into the lined basin. Damp down the edges of the crust and top with the pastry lid, making sure the edges are well sealed.

If your basin is an old-fashioned one and doesn't come with a lid, make one with foil or greaseproof paper, being sure to fold a pleat into the centre of it, to allow for any rising. Secure with string or a large elastic band. Place on the trivet in the pressure cooker if there's room, else put on a piece of tea towel (see page 14).

Add at least 5cm of hot water. Bring the water to the boil and put the cooker lid on, loosely, allowing the pudding to steam for 15 minutes without pressure. Close the lid, bring to high pressure and cook for 25 minutes. Allow to drop pressure naturally. Rest the pudding for 5 minutes, then turn out onto a plate and serve piping hot with cream or custard.

A Proper Custard

What use is a steamed pudding without proper custard? As a lot of custard-based desserts work in the pressure cooker I thought it stood to reason that proper custard, or *crème anglaise*, should too. It does – I worked out this quick version, which requires no preheating of milk or lengthy whisking of sugar and egg yolks, just a mix and 5 minutes of cooking time in the pressure cooker. The French often add just one coffee bean for depth of flavour so I tried it here – it does add a certain something.

You can also adapt this method if you want to make a quick custard as a base for ice cream. Simply substitute the quantities below with those in your ice cream recipe.

3 egg yolks
2 tbsp soft light brown sugar
300ml whole milk or milk/
  cream mixture

1 vanilla pod, split down
  the middle, or 1 tsp vanilla
  extract

1 coffee bean (optional)

Put the egg yolks and sugar in a bowl that will fit into your pressure cooker – I use a small Pyrex one. Whisk briefly just to amalgamate, then pour in the milk. Add the split vanilla pod or extract and the coffee bean if using. Cover with a piece of greaseproof paper and put in the pressure cooker. I usually put the bowl on a folded piece of tea towel to stop it rattling around. Add around 3cm of water to the cooker. Bring to high pressure and cook for 5 minutes. Fast release. Give the custard a quick stir – it should be smooth and slightly thickened.

Strain into a jug for immediate use or into a container for storage. Leave the vanilla pod in until you are ready to use the custard. If you are storing, keep in the fridge and cover with a piece of cling film to stop a skin from forming.

Rice Pudding

Rice pudding is one of those desserts that almost every cuisine seems to have embraced in some form or another. I stick to the traditional English version here, but feel free to vary it as much as you like, just make sure you use the same ratio of milk to rice.

100g short-grain rice (or use risotto rice)	100ml single cream	1 bay leaf
500ml milk	50g soft light brown sugar	Grating of nutmeg
	25g butter	

Put all the ingredients except the nutmeg into the pressure cooker, then grate some nutmeg over the top. Close the lid and bring to high pressure. Cook for 15 minutes, then allow to drop pressure naturally.

Stir briskly and leave to stand for a while with the lid on – the rice will continue to cook and gradually thicken further. If you want a skin on your rice pudding, transfer the contents to an ovenproof dish and grate over more nutmeg. Put under a hot grill until golden and dark brown in places.

You could also brûlée the pudding by sprinkling over some caster sugar and grilling it or using a blowtorch to caramelise it.

New York-Style Cheesecake with Salted Caramel

Apart from saving time and money, the main benefit of cooking a cheesecake in the pressure cooker is that you will not run the risk of a cracked top. I don't think I've ever managed to avoid that with a baked version, but it's never once happened since using the pressure cooker.

While it's possible to eat this warm, straight from the cooker, it is best to chill for at least 4 hours or overnight – it will improve the texture immeasurably. You can make individual cheesecakes too: I fill ring moulds, each one placed on a circle of foil, the sides folded up and secured with an elastic band to ensure no spillage, and put them in the steamer basket. They take around 8 minutes to cook.

If you are nervous about making the caramel sauce, you could substitute it with the *Dulce de Leche* (see page 201) instead – just flavour it with the same ingredients.

For the caramel	For the base	For the filling
100g granulated sugar	50g dark chocolate	400g cream cheese
150ml whipping cream	75g butter	150g soft light brown sugar
1 tsp vanilla extract	150g digestive biscuits	2 eggs
½ tsp sea salt		100ml soured cream
		1 tsp vanilla extract

To make the caramel, heat the sugar in a pan over a medium heat. When it starts to liquefy around the edges and turn a darker colour, gently begin swirling the pan around until the sugar has completely melted and is smoking a little. Immediately remove from the heat and pour in half the cream. It will splutter and bubble up just like overboiling milk. Stir briskly until the sugar and cream are amalgamated – you might need to put it over a gentle heat while doing this if some of the sugar hardens. Add the rest of the cream, the vanilla and salt. Put the pan in cold water to chill quickly then refrigerate until needed – the caramel should thicken as it cools.

Melt together the chocolate and butter for the base. I do this in a pan on a very low heat, but do use a *bain marie* (a bowl placed above, but not actually touching, simmering water) if you prefer. Whiz the biscuits in a food processor (or get rid of some aggression and bash them with a rolling pin), then add the melted butter and chocolate and mix. Press into a 20cm cake tin and put in the fridge to chill while you make the filling.

Cream together the cream cheese and sugar, then add the eggs, soured cream and vanilla. Pour over the biscuit base. Drop teaspoons of the caramel onto the cheesecake – most of it will sink and create 'pockets' of caramel in and under the filling. Reserve the rest of the caramel to serve separately with the cheesecake.

Put the trivet in the pressure cooker and pour in water until it almost reaches the top of the trivet. Make a foil handle (see page 15). Place the cake tin in the centre of the handle and lower onto the trivet. Fold the edges of the handle down, making sure that they don't touch or cover the cheesecake. Close the lid and bring to high pressure. Cook for 15 minutes then allow to drop pressure naturally.

Variations

Lime and ginger cheesecake

My in-laws prefer a zestier cheesecake. For them, I omit the vanilla, use gingernuts instead of digestives for the base, add the grated zest and juice of a lime to the filling and add finely chopped stem ginger and an optional tablespoon of rum to the caramel, along with just a pinch of the salt.

Cinnamon apple cheesecake

Add ½ teaspoon of ground cinnamon and a pinch each of ground cloves and ground allspice to the crushed digestives. Add these same flavours to the caramel, along with just a pinch of the salt and some apple brandy or Calvados, according to taste, if you have some. Finally, peel and dice a firm eating apple. Toss the apple pieces in a mixture of brown sugar with a touch of cinnamon, then stir this through the filling.

Blueberry and Orange Blossom Clafoutis

This combination came about completely by accident. I was making clafoutis with rhubarb and orange blossom water and was disappointed with the results – the rhubarb completely overwhelmed the orange blossom and was just too astringent a note for the fragrant, eggy clafoutis. As I had some batter left over, I cast around for an alternative, and spied a punnet of blueberries. I usually find that cooking diminishes the flavour of blueberries, so was surprised when it worked really well. Of course, there are any number of variations you can do here – blackberries and rose water is lovely, cherries or plums are wonderful with a little Kirsch added to the batter, as are chunks of peaches dusted in some ground amaretto biscuits.

You can make this in one shallow ovenproof dish, or several ramekins. The short cooking time reflects the fact that I like light, shallow clafoutis, rather than denser, high-sided versions.

Butter and brown sugar, to coat the dish

100g firm, just-ripe blueberries

Icing sugar, to dust

Whipped cream or crème fraîche, to serve

Splash of orange blossom water, to serve

For the batter

300ml double cream

½ vanilla pod, split lengthways

2 eggs

50g caster sugar

25g plain flour or ground almonds

1 tsp orange blossom water

Generously butter your dish or ramekins and sprinkle with brown sugar. Arrange the blueberries in the prepared dish.

Heat the double cream for the batter until almost boiling, then add the split vanilla pod. Leave to infuse until cool.

Whisk the eggs until frothy and completely broken up. Add the caster sugar and continue whisking. Fold in the flour until well combined, then add the cream infusion along with the orange blossom water. Pour the batter over the blueberries.

Cover with a circle of buttered greaseproof paper. Place your dish either on the trivet or on your upturned steamer basket. Pour boiling water into the cooker, making sure it doesn't reach the bottom of the dish. Close the lid and bring to full pressure. Cook for 5 minutes. Remove from the heat and allow to drop pressure naturally.

Remove the dish or ramekins from the pressure cooker. If you want the clafoutis slightly browned, put under a medium–hot grill for a couple of minutes. Dust with icing sugar and serve with whipped cream or crème fraîche, which is lovely if you have stirred some icing sugar and orange blossom water through it.

Chocolate Pots

These are perfect for easy entertaining, as they can be prepared ahead and just left to chill, ready to be eaten at your convenience. Regarding flavour, anything goes, as long as you keep the quantities of the core ingredients (cream, sugar, chocolate, egg yolks) the same. Just infuse the cream at the beginning with any aromatics you fancy. I take inspiration from all the creative and experimental chocolate makers, particularly L'Artisan du Chocolat, who introduced me to the tonka bean (a seed from the South American Cumaru tree, sweet with spicy undertones and often used as a headier, more complex substitute for vanilla) and to bizarre but delicious combinations such as banana and thyme. Also from Paul A. Young, who is not scared to mix chocolate with Marmite, or with port and stilton.

My particular favourites are basil, fennel seed, white chocolate with kaffir lime, gingerbread spices (use muscovado sugar if you want to try this one) and the one I use to illustrate this method – tonka bean and coffee.

300ml single cream

50g caster sugar

1 tonka bean or
  split vanilla pod

100g dark chocolate,
  broken into small pieces

1 tsp instant espresso powder
  (or 1 tbsp very strong espresso)

2 tsp rum (optional)

4 egg yolks

Butter, for greasing

Warm the cream and sugar until the sugar has dissolved, then add the tonka bean or split vanilla pod. When the mixture has almost reached boiling point, remove from the heat and leave to infuse for as long as possible, at least 30 minutes.

Return the cream to a low heat (remove the vanilla pod, if used) and add the dark chocolate. Stir until completely melted, and remove from the heat. Dissolve the espresso powder in a small amount of hot water and add to the mixture, then stir in the rum, if using. Whisk in the egg yolks, one at a time. Strain and pour into four ramekins. Cover with circles of buttered greaseproof paper.

Put the steamer basket in the pressure cooker, upturned. Pour in boiling water and put the ramekins on the basket. Close the lid and bring to high pressure. Cook for 5 minutes at high pressure, then fast release. Allow to cool a little, then serve warm or chilled.

Poached Peaches with Rosé and Rose Petals

I think it is sacrilege to cook a perfectly ripe peach – its honeyed fragrance is best enjoyed warmed by a late-afternoon sun, or at most, sliced and dropped into your glass of wine, as suggested by Elizabeth David in *Italian Food*. But sometimes peaches are not as sweet as they could be and this is a recipe for such times.

Here I attempt to infuse my below-par peaches with the spirit of late summer. A light syrup is made with a sweet rosé wine and honey, and infused with rose petals. If the rosé is too much of an extravagance, you can use water, but add a bit of sugar or more honey to make up for the loss of sweetness. The berries are optional, but a worthy addition; I especially like blackberries as their floral notes go very well with both peaches and rose.

You will probably have some of the syrup left over after serving. This is worth keeping in the fridge – it is delicious when added to sparkling wine or champagne for a version of Kir Royale.

400ml rosé wine

4 tbsp honey, preferably a light floral one

4 large firm peaches, halved and stoned

Handful of blackberries or blueberries (optional)

Handful of dried rose petals, plus a few more to serve

Ice cream or whipped cream, to serve

Heat the rosé in the pressure cooker and add the honey. Stir until thoroughly melted. Add the peaches, close the lid and bring to low pressure. Cook for 1 minute only, then release quickly. If you are using the blackberries or blueberries, add them and simmer for 1 minute – just enough time for them to soften and start bleeding into the liquid. Decant the contents of the pressure cooker into a bowl and crumble in the rose petals.

When the peaches are slightly cooled, remove the skins – they should just slide off. Return the fruit to the cooking liquid and leave to infuse until completely cool. Strain off the liquid, put in a pan or the pressure cooker and boil rapidly to reduce until it has become syrupy.

To serve, drizzle a couple of spoonfuls of the syrup over the peaches and blackberries, then sprinkle with rose petals. Eat with ice cream or a billowing pile of whipped cream.

Variations

Other poached fruits

Any fruits that need a fair amount of cooking are worth poaching in the pressure cooker. I will normally cook them in a light sugar syrup (use one third sugar, two thirds mixture of water/ other liquids), which can prolong the cooking time very slightly, but it's worth doing this way as the fruit will take on more flavour.

Pears

These are wonderful in a spiced, mulled red wine. Simmer together red wine with pared orange zest, cloves, cinnamon bark, mace, vanilla and sugar to taste. Add peeled pears and cook at high pressure. Firm pears will take 3 minutes if they are halved and cored, 5–6 minutes if they are left whole.

Try also cooking them in a sugar syrup flavoured with ginger wine, or with sweetened white wine with saffron – this will result in a quite stunning colour.

Quinces

These are best cooked in a syrup made entirely or partly with honey as this accentuates the same flavour in the fruit. I like using heady flavours such as rose, but I've also used lighter flavours – I once juiced some clementines that needed using up and added them to the syrup. Once I had cooked the quinces this syrup made a wonderful cordial. Quinces need cooking for anything between 15–30 minutes, depending on how firm they are. Open after 15 minutes in order to gauge how much longer they will need.

Plums and damsons

It's only really worth cooking these under pressure if they are stubbornly hard – bring to high pressure, immediately take off the heat and allow to drop pressure naturally. I like cooking plums in a syrup flavoured with port, ginger, star anise and perhaps a few Szechuan peppers. Add extra sugar after you have poached your plums, reduce down further and you have a lovely dipping sauce.

Dried fruit

The pressure cooker will soften any dried fruit very quickly, negating the need to pre-soak. Lovely desserts can be made with dried figs or prunes, which will take a minimum of 5 minutes at high pressure to cook. Try cooking figs with red wine, honey and thyme, or prunes with vanilla and (a current favourite) sweetened, smoky, chocolate-enhanced tea.

A Few Sweet Shortcuts

Dulce de Leche

A few people thought I was mad when I said that I was going to make *dulce de leche* in the pressure cooker, assuming it to be a very risky operation. It is not at all and it is incredibly easy. Normally, it takes anything between 2–4 hours of boiling a tin of condensed milk to get the required caramelisation, and you have to keep an eye on it to keep the steamer topped up with water. To do the same in the pressure cooker, simply put the tin on a piece of tea towel to stop it rattling around, surround with a few centimetres of water and cook at high pressure for 20 minutes. Leave it to drop pressure naturally and wait for it to cool down before you open the tin. This will create a thick, moreish *dulce de leche*. (For even more caramelisation, increase the cooking time by as much as another 10 minutes.)

You can also use home-made condensed milk or decant a tin of the same into a heatproof bowl, cover with a single layer of foil and cook for the same amount of time at high pressure. Then just give the mixture a thorough beating. The advantage of doing it this way is that you can flavour the milk with vanilla or anything else that takes your fancy. I especially like to add salt.

The uses of *dulce de leche* are many. The classic is banoffee pie – make a cheesecake base from 150g crushed digestive biscuits and 75g butter and chill. Spread over a whole can's worth (almost 400g) of *dulce de leche* and cover with sliced bananas (about three). Whip 250ml double cream and pile on top.

You can also use it in place of the caramel in the New York-Style Cheesecake on page 193, swirl it through home-made ice cream before you freeze it (I like digging out big lumps of it) or use it as a cake filling. I once filled a coconut carrot cake with *dulce de leche* that had toasted desiccated coconut stirred through it. Another time I stirred in some dark chocolate chips and spread the lot on bread for use in bread and butter pudding, which was particularly successful.

Softening Citrus Fruit

As you will see in the Preserves chapter (pages 203–17), you can soften whole citrus fruits incredibly quickly in the pressure cooker. While these are most useful for marmalade, you can also soften oranges for the classic Sephardic orange cake. Simply add as many oranges as you need to the pressure cooker, cover with water, and cook at high pressure for 10 minutes. Release pressure quickly.

Softening and Macerating Dried Fruit

If you want to plump up dried fruits to use in a cake or pudding, you can save time by heating them quickly in a pressure cooker. Small fruits, such as raisins and sultanas, can be scantly covered in liquid (water or tea, for example) and brought to high pressure, before immediately being taken off the heat. If they then need steeping in alcohol, drain them and add it – they will not need to be left overnight, but can be used by the time it takes you to make the cake.

I also cook fruit in a sugar syrup, before adding alcohol. This is useful to keep in the fridge for quick desserts – you can add the fruit to ice cream or cheesecake and stir the macerating liquid into cream for a very quick syllabub. Heat equal quantities of sugar and water together, then simmer until reduced by about one-third. Add the fruit, bring to high pressure and immediately remove from the heat and fast release. Add alcohol to taste. You can also add whole spices to the liquid – I often use both liquid and fruit to make a spiced rum and raisin ice cream.

Preserves

*'The best discovery
was that you can
make lovely, buttery
curds very quickly'*

It might seem strange to use the pressure cooker in preserve-making – after all, normally most of the cooking is done in a lidless pan and relies on a certain amount of evaporation to thicken the contents so that setting points can be reached. This is clearly something that cannot be done in the pressure cooker.

However, a lot of fruit and vegetables require a fair amount of cooking before they are soft enough to break down for sugar to be added to them. This includes orchard fruits, such as apples, pears and especially quinces, dried fruits such as figs, and foraged fruits such as crab apples and rose hips. The pressure cooker also makes very short work of softening citrus peel, so marmalade can be made much more quickly. For me, the best discovery was that you can make lovely, buttery curds very quickly, with minimal stirring. This was yet another thing that confounded me while researching this book!

There is one more element to preserving that I haven't explored in this chapter and that is home canning. This is hugely popular in America. Pressure canners are supersized pressure cookers that reach a higher temperature and PSI than a regular pressure cooker. They're used to bottle fruits and low-acid vegetables, soups, cooked beans and sauces (think tomato, or apple) – in fact, anything that is low in sugar and/or vinegar, which are normally essential for preserving. This negates the need for a lot of freezer space and is invaluable if you have an allotment or garden and grow your own fruit and vegetables, if you make visits to a pick-your-own or if you regularly make large quantities of any of the things listed above. Although there isn't yet a pressure canner available for sale in the UK, the price of a good one, plus shipping costs, from the US, is less than you'd pay for a top-quality pressure cooker here, so they're well worth thinking about buying. I'm hoping it won't be too long before they take off here – I certainly intend to make a pressure canner my next major purchase.

A few general tips for preserving:

1. You should always sterilise any jars in which you are going to store your preserves. This can be done either by running them through the hot cycle of the dishwasher or by washing them in hot, soapy water, rinsing thoroughly and drying out in a low oven.

2. If you can, use preserving sugar rather than granulated. It has larger crystals, so melts at a slower rate, which results in better clarity for your jellies and marmalades. Of course, this doesn't matter with chutneys.

3. If you are likely to make a lot of jellies, think about investing in a jelly bag and stand. This makes straining much easier. You can now get ones that click together very simply. Otherwise, line a large sieve with muslin and balance this over a bowl. Make sure that you scald the jelly bag or muslin in hot water before you start straining.

4. To check whether your jam or jelly has set, either use a jam thermometer, which you should place in your cooker/preserving pan as soon as you start boiling, or use the time-honoured method of dropping small amounts on a freezer-chilled saucer or plate. If the jam or jelly puckers and wrinkles when you touch it, it will have reached setting point.

5. Foam will form when you make jam or jelly. Don't worry about this – as soon as you turn off the heat, stir vigorously and it will disperse. If you want to minimise foam, add a small knob of butter when you start boiling.

6. When making jellies that have anything suspended in them (spices, herbs, finely chopped chilli), allow the jelly to cool in the pan for a few minutes, stirring regularly, before ladling into jars. Keep an eagle eye on your jars while the jelly is cooling; if you notice the contents have a tendency to rise to the top, stir again with a sterilised spoon.

7. All jams, jellies, chutneys, etc. will store indefinitely in cool, dark cupboards unless the recipe specifically states otherwise. Store in the fridge after opening.

Jams

Use the pressure cooker for any fruits that require more than a couple of minutes' simmering and that will also need a little liquid (water, juice or even alcohol) added to them. I would include most orchard fruits in this category (cook plums and apricots for 4 minutes, damsons for 5, quinces for 10–15). Of the soft fruits, only blackcurrants (4 minutes) and gooseberries (4–5 minutes) really benefit.

Pear and Ginger Jam

On its own, pear jam doesn't have a huge amount of flavour, but it really comes alive when partnered with stem ginger. I have been making this jam every year for the last ten and never tire of it. You could substitute the pear with marrow if you have a glut of them. It will require around the same amount of cooking time.

500g pears, peeled and cut into small dice	500g preserving sugar 2 tbsp lemon juice	100g drained stem ginger, rinsed and chopped very finely

Put the pears in the pressure cooker and add 200ml water. Close the lid and cook for 2 minutes then fast release. The pears should be soft but not completely broken down into a mush. Add the sugar, lemon juice and stem ginger. Cook over a low heat, stirring until the sugar has dissolved, then boil rapidly until setting point is reached (see page 205). Ladle into sterilised jars (see page 205).

Dried Fig and Orange Jam

A very quick and easy store-cupboard jam for when nothing else is at hand. It is excellent spread on nutty walnut breads with strong cheese. I like using this on the base of a bakewell tart, made with an orange-flavoured frangipane. You could also try making jam with dried apricots – especially good with a little almond liqueur such as Amaretto added at the end.

250g dried figs 250ml orange juice Grated zest of 2 oranges	Preserving sugar (around 500–750g, see method) Juice of 1 lemon	1 tbsp orange flower water or rum (optional)

Cut the hard stems off the figs and cut the fruit into quarters – this is easily done with a pair of scissors. Put the figs in the pressure cooker with the orange juice, zest and 200ml water. Close the lid and bring to high pressure. Cook for 10 minutes then allow to drop pressure naturally. The figs should be fairly soft.

Roughly purée the fig mixture in a food processor, then weigh it. Measure out between half and equal its weight in sugar, depending on how sweet you like it (I usually use about two-thirds). Put the fruit and sugar back into the pressure cooker or a preserving pan and heat gently, stirring constantly until the sugar has melted. Add the lemon juice, turn up the heat and boil rapidly until setting point is reached (see page 205). Remove from the heat and stir in the rum or orange flower water, if using. Ladle into sterilised jars (see page 205), seal and store in a cool, dark place. If you only used the minimum of sugar, you should refrigerate after opening.

Watermelon Rind Jam

A real waste not, want not preserve, this, that should appeal to the most parsimonious of people. It's also a talking point, as it's quite unusual in this country. I suggest you make it if you've tried the Moroccan Spiced Lamb with Mint and Watermelon Salad on page 75. You could also add a cinnamon stick, slices of ginger, or perhaps some fresh mint to this, right at the beginning when you soften the rind.

500g watermelon rind, peeled weight (see method)	Juice of 1 lime, plus two 5cm strips of pared zest	350g preserving sugar 50g strong-flavoured honey

First, pare off all the outer dark green skin of the watermelon rind and discard. Weigh the pale, green rind until you get the required amount. Cut the rind into thin strips. Put in the pressure cooker and cover in cold water, along with one of the lime strips. Close the lid and bring to high pressure. Cook for 10 minutes and fast release. The rind should be soft and translucent. For a smoother jam, you can purée the rind at this stage with a little of the cooking liquid, but this is not essential.

Drain the rind. Put the sugar in the pressure cooker and stir until it is dissolved. Add the honey, the remaining lime zest and the juice before returning the rind as well. Boil until setting point is reached (see page 205). Ladle into sterilised jars (see page 205), seal and store in a cool, dark place.

Quince Cheese

This is often known by its Spanish name, *Membrillo*. It's basically a jam that has been cooked down into a very stiff, sliceable paste and is absolutely delicious with strong cheeses. I also like a damson version, which requires less cooking time under pressure (5 minutes) and is excellent with cold meats.

This is the least time-consuming method. Normally it takes anything from 1½–3 hours for the quinces to cook down to the required softness. The pressure cooker takes between 10 and 15 minutes, depending on how ripe the fruits are.

1kg quinces	Preserving sugar (about 1.25kg, see method)	Juice of 1 lemon

Wash the quinces thoroughly. Cut into fairly small pieces, but there is no need to peel or core them. Put them in the pressure cooker and pour over 500ml water. Close the lid and bring to high pressure. Cook for 10 minutes and then allow to drop pressure naturally. You should now be able to mash the quinces very easily with the back of a wooden spoon. If not, bring to high pressure again and cook for a further 5 minutes.

When you are satisfied that your quinces are soft enough, purée the flesh with the water and push the resultant pulp through a coarse sieve. Measure the pulp into your pressure cooker or preserving pan, and add an equal amount of sugar. Also add the lemon juice. Stir this mixture over a very low heat, stirring constantly until the sugar has dissolved, then at regular intervals to make sure it doesn't stick on the bottom. The cheese will be ready when it is very stiff and you can stand your spoon up in it.

You can either spoon your quince cheese into sterilised jars (see page 205), or you can put it into sterilised and greased moulds, such as small terrine dishes. The moulds have the advantage in that you can later turn the cheese out and slice it, rather than having to spoon it out. Cover the moulds with greaseproof paper and keep in the fridge.

Variation

Jelly sweets

You can also follow Jane Grigson's recommendation in her *Fruit Book* and turn your quince or damson cheese into sweetmeats. Line baking trays with oiled cling film, spread the cheese out onto it and leave to dry overnight. Then cut into shapes and roll in granulated sugar. You could also mix a little citric acid with the sugar in order to get a bit of a fruit-pastille fizz.

Grapefruit Marmalade

You can save a huge amount of time by using the pressure cooker for marmalade. Normally, you would need to simmer the fruit for at least 2 hours for it to become soft enough, but with a pressure cooker, 10 minutes is normally sufficient, 15 at the outside. You can use this recipe as a template for any other citrus marmalades, especially for Seville oranges, which are in season around January. But I have a nostalgic attachment to grapefruit marmalade as it's the one we made most when I lived in the Caribbean.

Most marmalade recipes use twice the amount of sugar to fruit, but I like my grapefruit marmalade quite sour so I use equal amounts. If you prefer yours sweeter, increase the amount of sugar anywhere up to double the amount of fruit.

This recipe makes rather a lot of marmalade; for variety, you can split it up once setting point has been reached and add all kinds of things – chopped stem ginger, rum or whisky, or a mixture of spices (star anise, cloves) that will suspend in the jelly along with the citrus peel.

1.5kg grapefruit	Juice of 1 large lime	1.5kg preserving sugar

Wash the fruit thoroughly in warm water. This is particularly important if your fruit has been waxed, as warm water will dissolve this. Put the whole fruit in the pressure cooker with 1.5 litres of water. Seal down and bring to high pressure. Cook for 10 minutes, then remove from the heat and allow to reduce pressure naturally. The skin of the fruit should be soft enough to be easily pierced with the handle end of a wooden spoon.

Remove the fruit from the water and leave until it is cool enough to handle. Do not discard the liquid! Cut the grapefruits in half and scoop out the contents: pulp, membranes, seeds and all, and push as much liquid as you can through a sieve back into the pressure cooker. Tie anything that is left behind into some muslin, for easy removal later, and put in the pressure cooker. It's important to include these bits, as they are full of pectin and will help your marmalade to set.

Meanwhile, shred the peel with a sharp knife. How thickly you do this is a matter of personal preference. Generally, I slice each fruit lengthways into quarters and cut very finely on the diagonal across each segment. Add the shredded peel to the strained liquid, along with the lime juice and the sugar.

Put the pressure cooker over a low heat and stir until all the sugar has dissolved. You will be able to feel when this is done as the wooden spoon will no longer feel scratchy on the base of the pan, and the mixture will be much more liquid. Turn up the heat and bring to the boil, and keep boiling fairly rapidly, and stirring regularly, until setting point is reached. This will probably take around 10 minutes. Remove the marmalade from the heat and stir briskly to disperse any scum that may have gathered at the top. Leave to cool for a while, stirring regularly to make sure that the shredded peel remains evenly distributed, then ladle into sterilised jars (see page 205), seal and store in a cool, dark place.

Lemon Curd

I found this recipe in an old book by Dianne Page called *Pressure Cookery Properly Explained*, in which I was surprised to see a recipe for curd. It works like a dream, saving a lot of time that would normally be spent stirring away at a hot stove. I make this in a Pyrex bowl, but any heatproof dish that fits into the pressure cooker will do.

There are many variations to this. When I worked in the Caribbean, we made curds primarily with lime, but also with sour orange (try using Seville oranges when they become available in January) or with passion fruit. You could try juicing gooseberries or blackcurrants, or even adding other aromatics – I once successfully added a couple of heads of lavender to lemon curd.

4 eggs	Grated zest of 2 lemons	75g butter
450g caster sugar	150ml lemon juice	

Beat the eggs together in a Pyrex bowl then add the sugar. Mix thoroughly, then add all the other ingredients. Cover the bowl with greaseproof paper and balance it on the trivet inside the pressure cooker, using a foil handle for easy removal (see page 15). Pour water into the pressure cooker, making sure it doesn't reach the bowl. Close the lid and seal, then bring to high pressure. Cook for 10 minutes then release naturally.

You may find that a layer of butter has formed on top – stir vigorously for a minute to combine everything, then push through a sieve. Decant into sterilised jars (see page 205), seal and store in the fridge.

Jellies, Savoury and Sweet

Fruits such as apples, crab apples, gooseberries and quinces make wonderful bases for herbed and spiced jellies, they just need a bit of softening first, something for which the pressure cooker is ideal. These fruits have the additional benefit of being very rich in pectin, so should set easily without recourse to manufactured pectin. The jellies are very useful for adding to gravies and sauces, or simply for serving with cold meats and cheeses. I like to serve a selection with deep-fried Brie, Camembert or goat's cheese.

Herb Jellies

| 1kg cooking apples, crab apples, quinces or gooseberries | Herbs, spices, flowers (see variations opposite) | Plenty of preserving sugar (see method) |

Roughly cut up your chosen fruit and put in the pressure cooker, pips, skin and all. Cover with water – I use half the amount of water to fruit if it is very ripe, or closer to equal quantities if the fruit is very hard. Add your chosen herbs, spices or flowers. Close the lid and bring to high pressure. Cook gooseberries for 3 minutes, apples and crab apples for 5 minutes and quinces for 10–15 minutes. Allow to release pressure naturally.

Mash the fruit up a little with the back of a spoon, then put the entire contents of the pressure cooker into a jelly bag or muslin-lined sieve and suspend over a bowl. Leave to strain, preferably overnight. Do not attempt to speed things along by pushing it through, as this will result in a cloudy jelly.

Measure how much liquid you have. For every 600ml liquid, add 450g sugar. Cook over a low heat, stirring until the sugar has dissolved, then boil rapidly until setting point is reached (see page 205). Stir to disperse any scum and allow to cool slightly before adding any additional chopped herbs, flowers or spices to your jelly.

After 5 minutes, stir vigorously for a couple of minutes to stop any additions from floating to the top. Leave for a further 5 minutes to make sure they are still evenly distributed and stir again if they aren't. Ladle into sterilised jars (see page 205) and seal. Store in a cool, dark place.

Variations

Gooseberry and mint

Add 1 tablespoon of cider vinegar to the liquid when you add the sugar.

Apple and tarragon

Add 50ml white or rosé wine at the beginning with the apples.

Quince and rose or geranium

Add a few rose petals or geranium leaves when you cook the quinces.

Thyme, sage, rosemary or lemon balm

These all make lovely herb jellies combined with apple.

Scotch Bonnet Jelly

Follow the instructions given for Herb Jellies opposite, but include a red pepper and a Scotch bonnet pepper, both seeded and roughly chopped, and a sprig of thyme when you cook the apples. Before ladling into the jars, add two finely chopped Scotch bonnets. This jelly is good warmed through with a little red wine and used as a dip for any kind of fritter.

Sloe and Apple Jelly

I forage for sloes and crab apples every year – they crop up all over the place. I used to find them easily when I lived in Norfolk and was pleasantly surprised to stumble across some in West London too. I often use sloes for vodka or gin, but sometimes keep some back to make this jelly – or I wait until I can strain off the alcohol and use them in the jelly afterwards. Follow the instructions given for Herb Jellies opposite, but use 500g sloes and 500g crab apples or cooking apples, along with 1 teaspoon of crushed juniper berries, which should be added right at the beginning.

Rose Petal Jelly

A sweet jelly, this time, courtesy of Joanna Cary whose blog 'An English Kitchen' is full of beautifully written recipes. As she is careful to point out, make sure that you use unsprayed roses, as those sold for decorative purposes are not suitable for human consumption. Go for a rose with a strong scent – red and dark pink ones tend to work very well. If fresh rose petals are out of the question, you can also use dried rose petals, available in most Middle Eastern grocery stores. A 50g bag should be sufficient for the quantities given. If you want to add other flavours to this jelly, I recommend a handful of lemon balm, or some blackberries.

1 litre rose petals, a handful reserved	Juice of 2 lemons	1kg preserving sugar

Put the rose petals and 1 litre of water in the pressure cooker and close the lid. Bring to high pressure and cook for 5 minutes. Allow to drop pressure naturally.

Do not be worried by the sight that greets you. The rose petals will have lost their colour and the water will be a murky brown, but will also be redolent with the scent of roses. Leave the rose petals to cool in the liquid and then strain. Discard the petals (or reserve to add later) and keep the water.

When the rose-infused liquid has cooled, add the lemon juice. The liquid will miraculously turn a bright pink. Return this to the pressure cooker or a preserving pan and add the sugar. Proceed as with the Herb Jellies on page 212. You can shred the reserved rose petals and add them at the end, if you like.

Garden Vegetable Chutney

This uses up all those things that become difficult to use up towards the end of summer – courgettes or marrows, green tomatoes, cooking apples – and can of course be varied enormously. The quantities are large because it makes sense to produce a lot of this at once – it keeps for years, after all. Note also that the weights given are after any peeling, coring, etc. The ginger adds a good warmth, but feel free to also add some chilli flakes if you like.

5cm piece of root ginger, roughly chopped

1 tsp allspice berries

1 tsp coriander seed

2 tsp black peppercorns

1 mace blade

4 cloves

1kg courgettes, marrows or other squash, diced

1kg green tomatoes (I like tomatillos if I can get them), skinned, seeded and diced

500g onions, finely chopped

2 garlic cloves, finely chopped

500g peeled cooking apples, cored and diced

600ml cider vinegar

1 tsp salt

500g soft light brown sugar

Put all the spices in a piece of muslin and tie with string. Put the vegetables, garlic and apples in the pressure cooker. Add the vinegar, the spice mix bag and the teaspoon of salt. Close the lid and bring to high pressure. Cook for 10 minutes, then fast release.

Add the sugar and stir over a low heat until it is completely dissolved. Simmer slowly, stirring regularly, until the chutney has reduced and thickened – a good indication is if you can clear a path at the bottom of the cooker with your wooden spoon. Leave to cool for around 15 minutes and then give it another stir. Decant into a sterilised bottle (see page 205) and leave somewhere cool and dark for at least 6 weeks to allow the flavours to develop.

Onion Marmalade

This is a dark, sticky, caramelised marmalade, great with strong cheese or as an accompaniment to a spicy sausage. I also like this marmalade made with a mixture of red wine and sherry vinegars, and flavoured with lots of juniper. The pressure cooker comes in very handy here, as it speeds up the first part of the cooking process. It would normally take a good 45 minutes to get the onions soft enough to proceed, but here it takes only 10 minutes.

1kg onions, thinly sliced
375ml malt vinegar
4 dried bay leaves
375g soft light brown sugar
2 large thyme sprigs
Salt and freshly ground pepper

For the pickling spice
4 cloves
1 tsp allspice berries
1 tsp white peppercorns
½ tsp mustard seed
½ tsp coriander seed

Generous pinch of chilli flakes
1 mace blade
5cm piece of cinnamon stick

Put the onions in the pressure cooker with the vinegar. Lightly crush all the pickling spices together, roughly breaking up the mace and cinnamon. Add to the pressure cooker along with the bay leaves. Close the lid, bring up to pressure and cook for 10 minutes. Fast release. The onions should be soft and translucent.

Add the sugar to the pressure cooker along with the thyme and some salt and pepper. Stir over a low heat until all the sugar is dissolved, then cook at a fast-paced simmer until the marmalade is dark, thick and syrupy, stirring every so often.

Seal into sterilised jars (see page 205). This is best left for at least a couple of weeks before eating and should store indefinitely. *(See photograph, overleaf.)*

Acknowledgements

I expected that the writing of this book would be quite a lonely task but instead was overwhelmed by the amount of help and support I was given by so many people. In particular Stella O'Brien, Maunika Gowardhan, Joanna Cary, Kerstin Rodgers, Erin McGann and Fiona Bird were very generous with advice, encouragement, testing and often simply the opportunity for a good brain storm. Thanks also to Fiona Beckett for offering a calm voice when I started to panic and to Laura Pazzaglia of website hippressurecooking.com who was always happy to talk through ideas and who allowed me to use her bottle top tip for steaming eggs!

Thank you to Imogen Fortes and Sarah Lavelle. You are brilliantly sympathetic and skilful editors and it has been a pleasure working with you both.

Thank you to my agent Clare Hulton for taking me on and being incredibly patient and supportive when dealing with all my first book wobbles, and to Nick Coffer for the introduction! Thanks also to Dan Jones and Emma Marsden for making the photoshoot such an enjoyable experience.

I'm very grateful to Susan Smillie at the *Guardian* for giving an unknown, unpublished writer a break. Many people have helped me since I started writing about food, but none more than Tim Hayward and Hannah Norris, who give me regular fixes of unfailing humour, straight talking and indispensable common sense advice.

Thanks go to Andreia for getting me all fired up about pressure cookers in the first place – who would have thought it would lead to this? Thanks too to Mama Ali for all the recipes – we all love your food!

Much love and gratitude to my parents – my mother is a wonderful cook and I'm lucky that she had the time and patience to pass her expertise on to me. During the writing of this book, she offered endless encouragement and bought herself a new pressure cooker so she could help out with testing. Fortunately, she's now a convert. Thanks also to my father who has spent the past 20 years or so encouraging me to write.

This would have been a much harder process without the love, patience and whole-hearted support from Shariq. Heartfelt thanks and love to him and to my other favourite mouths to feed, Lilly and Adam.

Index